MYSTERY BABYLON
REVEALED

MYSTERY BABYLON

REVEALED

BILLY WILSON

MYSTERY BABYLON REVEALED

iUniverse books may be ordered through booksellers or by contacting:

iUniverse
1663 Liberty Drive
Bloomington, IN 47403
www.iuniverse.com
1-800-Authors (1-800-288-4677)

ISBN: 978-1-5320-2034-6 (sc)
ISBN: 978-1-5320-2035-3 (e)

Library of Congress Control Number: 2017938047

Print information available on the last page.

iUniverse rev. date: 04/10/2017

FOREWORD

This is a book of many, many truths, therefore hated by any and all evil, in any form. You can only keep truth out of the battle by covering it up and ignoring it, only then evil can prevail. This book is written in a effort to bring as much truth to light as possible. Hoping you have the stimulate to read it.

By: Billy G. Wilson

CHAPTER 1

CRAZY TALK

God's Spirit is about life, this book is about God's Spirit.

Before the end of the world comes, God's teaching tells us the entire world will be divided into two kinds of people. Them that have God's Spirit, and them that belong to the Mystery Babylon Whore, of Revelations, Ch. 17. God verily teaches there are words that are truth and there are words that are lies. Then there are many words that are slanted, perverted, confusing, and running back and forth in between. God has said plainly we will answer for every idle word we speak.

I take that to be the reason for much Bible cautioning on being slow to speak, swift to hear, and be careful how we do both. When we are speaking words, we are sowing seeds. I can hardly see any other definition for it. We are told to sow nothing but godly seed and we will reap nothing but godliness.

If a word can be found in the Bible, it is a spiritual word, if not it is a carnal word. Be very careful how they are sowed. The way we are reaping is the way we are sowing, otherwise we are reaping someone else's harvest and to leave it alone as much as possible, and speak truth.

Paul, says to be quite to mind our own business, this is good advice but many times we don't have a choice. Someone will push it over on us and make it our business. In that case God says for us to handle it. I kind of call that getting caught in the middle. In a sense, Christians are always caught in the middle. I believe that is where God has called us. I will not use that as an excuse for not doing my part, and minding my business God called me into. I try to handle it knowing I will answer to God first for every word I use.

God is not there just to measure and judge us but also there to help us if we love truth and will listen to him. You will be saved and have help in time of need. This, is why, it is a must for us to be in Jesus' name, which is in his Spirit. He is mighty hard to beat when he is on your side. If you are careful you will get into the habit of depending on him. There is no better place to be.

A carnal spirit cannot be in the Spirit of God and cannot stand up to truth. Truth is Jesus, and Jesus is truth, and carnal cannot handle truth. If you put truth up against a carnal spirit or person, he will instantly get mad and belligerent. If he thinks he is bigger than you, it might be advisable to get you a club. Easy way to know what spirit you are up against. When they get in your face and jump up and down calling you names and telling you how crazy and stupid you are; it is hard for me to keep the victory and have pity on them. I read where God himself reacts to anger.

He has told me to be angry but sin not, and don't let the sun go down upon my wrath. I believe that insinuates to get it settled, before sundown, if possible. He has also told me there is a time to kill and a time to make alive. I've always said I can and may end up with my back-side kicked and nothing else. But usually I can get things settled and find out quickly where I stand. I already know where I stand with God. Then I can feel better about it and maybe I can handle it correctly. I've been called crazy by a lot of people; they are entitled to their opinion. Just be careful about getting in my face and pushing me around to tell me about it. I might just go a little bit crazy. I've been known to. I don't mean that to sound boastful or a threat, just being honest, that is just me. Call it one of my weak sides if you like. I have several more.

I have found about anybody that speaks straight and truth to a selfish carnal minded person, is just about always considered a little on the crazy side. After looking up the word crazy in the English dictionary, I found it gave only one short definition out of maybe a dozen, that referred to a diminished mind. The rest referred to such things as scattered, deranged, no shape. One even said, fuzzed up. So, I can see how someone speaking truth to a carnal mind that cannot handle, truth, which is Christ himself, would receive us as a little bit crazy. I only then saw why God gave me the title of "Crazy Talk" to name this book when I started it.

God has not only taught us to know our self but also judge our self. If we our found to be wrong, to confess, repent and pay restitution if owed, but to stand firm on what is truth. This will just about settle any problem, if it doesn't then I believe it is on the other one. Then you might ask him how he wants to settle it. Careful, or there you all go again. This is what I mean by a fleshly (Or carnal) spirit is never satisfied. I read where Billy the Kid said, "Some people you just have to kill to get them out of your way." I guess that was his solution to that problem. You must make your own choses. We will live and die and be judged by our choses, this is gospel.

I preach hard, every word is what it is, by where you are looking at it from. So, I suppose crazy is no exception, your choice as to how you want to look at it. I would never attempt to pass judgment on Billy the Kid, God can do that and will. But I have always admired the guts and boldness in his character that writers have always depicted it with.

The word crazy is not in the Bible, which means it is a carnal word, not a spiritual one. The definition for the word in the carnal, says it refers to being deranged or no shape, scattered, unsound, out of the ordinary. I believe Satan has been shifting what mankind accepts as ordinary, to maybe what some calls more like, radicalized, another word in the carnal language. I believe "Devil-possessed" could be the most correct word God has used to describe them both. Or, beside oneself, I think it kind of implies out of one's mind. It seems that crazy is becoming more the ordinary than a sound mind. God did say the day will come when people will not endure sound doctrine, so they like to call sound minds crazy. Makes them feel better about themselves.

That brings up another subject to me, language. God confused the world's language at the building of the tower of Babel. Up until then, the world spoke one and the same language. I do not believe he left the same language that he said the whole earth spoke, up until then, for any small group and took it from everyone else. That just does not sound like God. He did say he took it from the whole earth. Every person and every creature had to learn a new way of talking among themselves. That had enough in common among them to hold them together long enough to learn a unified Language. Our languages have remained with the same confusion until today, only worse. As everybody's language has grown and not always in the same way and direction, and new ones are being started. The same as everything else God did in the Bible, God exclaimed why he did it.

With one language, man was becoming as one and starting to organize against God and nothing would be restrained unto them. I am sure God was not worried about man moving him over and taking his seat, as man is always trying to do. But he could have just about stopped God's plan to reconcile a portion of humankind back to himself, out of the ones that were somewhat worthy. All of mankind was fast becoming eternally lost with no hope, being as one without God.

As language (Communication) is one of the most vital things to binding people into one. God took their language away from the earth, to divide them up. Confusion has worked until today, starting the first day and gotten more effective ever since. Man, has just recently done absolutely, amazing things with the communication among men, but can only survive death if he can get back into communication with God, which is a Spirit. God is truth, and can accept nothing but truth, since that is all that he is, no part of a lie can be added to him.

Man, had fallen from God to a carnal level, and cannot accept truth but is completely a lie himself, apart from God he is considered dead. God has tried to save man by adding truth to him but truth and carnal will not mix no better than oil and water. Man, would have to learn complete obedience to God in order-to become one with him, in principle, purpose, Spirit or anything else. God accepts nothing but truth, no part of a lie can be added to him and he will add nothing but truth to us.

This constitute quite a problem for carnal man. God has tried everything that a man could come up with to reconcile man back to God; the patriarch, the twelve sons of Joseph, the judges, princes, kings, the beast of a heathen government, and many prophets. I believe any way you can think of; God has tried it. He probably got more mileage with the heathen government but they kept getting more and more corrupt and none of them worked well. There will have been a total of seven of them by the time it is over. Too many people were falling through the cracks and being eternally lost while only a very small percent was being gleaned from all mankind, to be reconciled back into the Spirit.

Jesus loved mankind so much; God devised a plain for Jesus to volunteer to pay the price for all of them that would volunteer to be born again into his spiritual body and love it. They would be saved and could be accepted by him into eternity with God, as a brother to his begotten Son. The rest of them being separated. Knowing that someone that loved themselves more than truth and righteousness would be miserable in eternity with him. Carnal flesh had to die out. If I can understand my Bible correctly, we will receive a final weeding out even after the battle of Armageddon. He did say he would end up with a tried and proven people. Like everything else he has said, I believe him.

Jesus became born into flesh, grew up into the flesh as one of us, being tempted as you and I, learned by his suffering. Gave his own body for a sacrifice for all mankind that would receive him as a savior.

Jesus chose to Give the English-speaking people the one spiritual language that could unite us all back to one again. The language is Jesus himself. One in agreement with God the Father, Jesus the Son, both in the form of the Kingdom of God by the Holy Ghost. Big enough to have room for every person that would accept a new birth. But it was still a completely spiritual thing and a little confusing to the flesh, as anything between a lie and truth is confusion.

England sought him for it with a whole heart, and accepted the spiritual writing of it and an agreement to not add another word to it. Not even another English word, even one that has been added to the English language since, and certainly not from another carnal language of the world. And not to take ought from any word he used in the Word of God; which was Jesus himself, just made into another form.

Jesus gave himself to mankind in the form of an authorized written book. This is the reason the Bible is such a sacred book, Jesus is its entire contents. Spiritually written, spiritually discerned with no other way through or around it. We never had such a thing given to mankind until around the year AD sixteen-hundred, on our calendar. I will certainly be writing more in this book about that.

Now you can start an argument from any direction you chose, but it will instantly tell God and me, you do not believe the Bible, if you cannot believe what I just wrote. For it is the Bible. I promise you if you read this book, you will be reading more about God's language all through it, about how we are called into one. Everybody comes into the Kingdom of God the same way and it would do you no good to read it in the Bible, if you can't believe it. It says you will be eternally lost if you don't believe the record God gave us of his Son. You need to read your Bible, the one God said he wrote. Again, it is your chose.

Better yet, get someone sent by the Spirit of God to read it to you. They are hard to find, so you will need to seek for the help of the Spirit of God for yourself. God has not chosen to force anybody to accept him in any way, but has made an easy plan for anyone that desires to learn his language and communicate with him and the rest of his body here on this earth. The complete plan of God is set up for the Word of God to be brought to any person by something or someone with the Spirit of God. No one can be saved if the Spirit of God cannot draw you to him. We are ordered to help one another, guided by the Bible which is Jesus Christ.

He does not want any part of a carnal confused language, called carnal reasoning, mixed into his language. He is aware we speak to one another in a carnal language, but has written the Bible to explain any carnal word in the world, if studied and shared. While the carnal language cannot explain the Bible but very little if any. Anyone must learn it from someone sent from and by the Holy Spirit making it to where, if you don't seek God's Spirit, you don't have it. He has ordered all his people to be apt to teach, and to answer any questions ask to him about the hope he has in him. Keep in mind one is supposed to be walking in the Spirit. If he cannot answer him, he is to take him to someone who can, and do some studying for himself and maybe he can answer the next one that ask him. They must all be able to hear and speak the spiritual language or someone will be left out.

One is instructed to speak nothing but truth to one's neighbor, this is meant to spread the Kingdom of God without lies being involved in it in any way. There are no lies in God's language. There is no negative or tearing down truth in the Word of God, it is for building up the truth. Two truths will always agree together. Therefore, Satan hates anything about truth, he is all about lies and tearing down, nothing else in him. Nothing but another lie will enforce or help hold up a lie, then God considers it to be a lie also. It should be easy for true Christians to recognize Satan, he is a liar and the father of lies. But false Christians seem to love lies, for they are in the same business and can walk arm and arm together in agreement with him, very well. God will have no part with either one. Are they going to wait until judgment to see and believe what God has said? No marvel that Jesus said there is going to be so few of them. It is because there is going to be so few of them.

Every Christian is instructed to always be alert, for Satan never sleeps and is always seeking whom he may devour. He is seeking for anyone he can tempt and lead off track any amount. Just a slight angle will lead completely off track with a little time. God has called that being devoured. Satan's time is getting shorter, he knows it and is working overtime with all his imps to devour all he can before his time is up. I believe he has more time left than most of us, for sure. But not more time than our seed. God has told us to sow Godly seed and keep his Word alive on this earth, through our seed. Seems to me we are letting him down. When his Word goes down so does the country. His Word is the strength of God for anything that has it and believes it.

I intend to try to explain as many of my statements as I can before I finish this book. Try to hang on, with an interest, I believe anybody can learn much. Keep in mind, I am not infallible, but the Word of God is, God does not make mistakes. The only thing I read where he repented of making, was mankind. He could snap his finger and there would not be even a memory left of us, but Moses and the priesthood stood in the gap for us.

The prophets, judges, princes, kings, and so many, stood in the gap for the few that would hear and obey until Jesus came and was born into the flesh and gave his carnal body for all of us. Replaced the earthly priesthood and sent back the Holy Ghost for everybody that would be born again into it. Because he loved the few that would become one with him. Made it plain that this would be the last opportunity offered to man. If one cannot believe that, where is his salvation coming from? God has said we must believe him. There is no other way. I believe if there could have been a better way to have accomplished everything God wanted to accomplish, God would have used it.

God poured out his spirit to mankind for the first time at *Pentecost.* When Peter used, the key Jesus left him to open the door to the kingdom of God. It must have been one of the biggest events in the history of mankind. Some denominations do not even believe in it. I'll never understand. Where are they ever going to find any hope when Jesus says, there is no other way. Just except the Spirit of God.

CHAPTER 2

THE BIBLE IS COMPLETELY A SPIRITUAL THING

The Bible is the Spirit of God in the form of a book. Put together by seventy plus men using a very stringent set of rules to qualify any writings in the world to fit perfectly. Before they could be entered as authenticated scripture. Mostly that it was referred to by Jesus or one of his disciples for verification; and close to thirty other qualifications. When it was completed, Jesus said it was him, with his power.

A book of revelations given to God's prophets, kings, princes and men chosen by God to reveal the plan of God to redeem his people back to him. After the whole human race fell from him by choice and became carnal (Apart from the Spirit) in the garden. Revealed in a way that is hidden to anybody that does not humble himself, believe, love, trust and fear God. And is not wise in his own conceit. Only God could do such a thing.

We must study his Word the way, and manner he told us to, and believe, to receive any understanding given by his Spirit. This includes establishing every Word of God by the mouth of two and three witnesses from the Word of God. Believing it will result in, being born into the Spirit of God, sent back by both him and his son, Jesus Christ. Called the Holy Ghost and referred to as a born-again experience, by Peter and Jesus. It is called becoming a new creature, by the apostle Paul, called salvation by all of them, and the prophets.

This was done when Jesus, the Word, came and full filled his part in the whole law concerning the priesthood, and brought in the Kingdom of God, which is Spirit and Truth, Light and Life. A complete new thing given to man and replaced the old and earthy priesthood, even though it seems that every, God claiming, man organization, seems to think they inherited the old priesthood all to themselves. I believe, I read where God said he done away with it by replacing it with Jesus Christ. Which is in the form of the Spirit of God and is to live inside each one of us that will accept him by a new birth. And will allow him to have complete charge of our vessels. There is to be no division in his body. Called becoming one with Jesus Christ.

You should be able to see plainly why Jesus said there will be so few of them. God preformed this of course just like he had prophesied, and promised mankind he would do. It takes the Spirit to see it, or anything else about God's Word, it is Spirit.

We are told that the engrafted Word, which is Jesus, can save your soul. The only Word I know that has the Spirit's seal of the approval of the Lord Jesus Christ and his apostles and has every word of it backed up and proven a million times, is the Bible. I have often said, I believe America will be the most inexcusable people that will stand before God in judgement. If you cannot rise above the carnal you cannot see one word of it for your own.

We are to study the Bible prayerfully, which means much meditation day and night and without doubt. To read the Bible any other way you are not apt to get anything out of it unless it just falls on you. The Bible ask, "How can we believe if we have not heard; and how can we hear without a preacher; and how can he preach if he hasn't been sent?" All Christians are called to be apt to teach. If we don't study, like Jesus said over and over for us to do. We will not be able to do a lot of teaching; about no explaining, not even to our own children.

When our children have not been taught, what do we have? Just what we have got, is what we will have. We have a Godless world, without the Bible. The Bible is the book that Jesus said every word in it would be fulfilled before the end of the world came. Notice how old fashion, "*The end of the world sounds?*"

When I was a boy around seventy years ago, it was a common topic because more people studied their Bible. Every home had one. A whole lot less of them could read, almost none of them could read well. But all of them knew the end of the world was coming and was greatly concerned about it. Most of them went to church to hear about it. All of them heard and listened about what was being preached at church whether he attended or not and the kids feared and respected the church house and things about it. That was the way they were trained. Today the younger generation cannot visualize such a society; no manner what part of the country they were raised in. Satan has cluttered up our time. To speak of the end of the world puts a smile on anybody's face. We old timers are not the ones that are foolish; the ones with the smiles and unconcern are the fools.

Do you suppose our children, not being raised up in the fear and admonition of the Lord just might be the biggest problem the world has today? I think so, and very strongly. This world's problems rest on its schools and homes and what they are teaching. Our schools in this country, started out being an extension of the homes and parents. Controlled by the parents with the Bible for the guide book for the entire curriculum. When they had a problem or a disagreement the Bible was accepted as sufficient to settle any problem. The Bible was believed and feared.

Mystery Babylon, being built and operated by government schools, realized they.could only gain complete control of this great country by controlling its schools and curriculum to our children. Later found out that if we kept our Bibles they could not ever control our country, so our Bibles must go. Now, some of the most ungodly teaching parents I know, are ones that have gone to college, the longer, the worse (Would you allow me to use "worser"? I didn't think so, might side track one of your kids and cause them to go wrong, I apologize). *sic*

The people who did not want to accept the simple responsibility of their children and voted and campaigned for a government run by Mystery Babylon, who wanted to own and control the children to raise them to accept the government that was so much smarter than their parents, or any God. And could offer them so much more materially, if they could come into control of all the parents and everything they had materially.

They wanted to retain the authority, to make the parents responsible, to raise the children like the government wanted them raised, or they would be put in jail. Even to teaching them the government was their God. No other God could be taught to them or even told about to them. We have become so busy and occupied with serving ourselves we have no time for God or our children, look where it has lead us. This is what we got.

The parents think they got a bargain. Mystery Babylon, with its False Prophets, told us we did, now who can argue with her? Maybe that is what God meant when he said of the last days, there in Isaiah, that the women would rise and rule over you and your children would be your princes and oppressors. He was obviously talking to America more than any other country on earth. Maybe, the only country starting out, rooted and grounded fully in God's Word Now we have some of the highest educated, and perverted minds I believe you can find in the pages of history making our laws, running our country, teaching and raising our children when they cannot tell, when a child is born, if it is a male or a female. They must wait until they are eighteen years, or so, old and ask them how they feel. It doesn't count how God made you, it is how you feel. If anyone cannot see this, I believe they are just as dumb as our people in Washington DC, that Mystery Babylon sent us to elect from. Isn't that the way it adds up?

One of Hillary Clinton's campaign promises was to "Build an international school to teach some people how to run this country." What do you suppose she had in mind? And why did it need to be an international school? Can we not build a school in our own country to train people to run this country? I was thinking that was one of the things our schools were supposed to be doing. Does she think we need to build a school in the Middle East to teach Muslims how to run our country? Or maybe build it in Germany or Italy. I'm for sure I'm dumb, but I would like somebody to explain farther to me just what she had in mind.

I can rest assured that Hillary Care was one thing, as it included the bulk of it was designed to help the Muslims and illegal aliens and only them. Another thing she stated she wanted to teach was to put our country completely under the United Nations; including our military power; to oversee our complete court system; take charge of all federal lands and national parks; approve all our curriculum taught in our schools. Of course, to disarm all citizens except them that were approved and working for the so called, Democratic UN government. And the United States were to finance it of course. It already does, no change necessary there.

I considered it obvious, her and Bill, "The most popular man on earth," had big plans, for her to move into the president's seat, and Bill to move over and take charge of the UN, basically they would be running the world. The U.S. treasury was the only place they had to get the money from to buy that position. Now Obama is plaining on that seat. At the price of twenty trillion dollars. But the world is not as stupid as most our selfish reprobate minded, gullible, something for nothing, God hating, American voters. That love to believe a lie and are dammed. Read Romans, chapter one.

I would prefer the United Nations take charge of our country, before Hillary or Obama or any Democrat I could name. You would think we would have found that out by now, but reprobate minded people can't ever stop believing lies without a very high expense tag for us attached to it, for our grandchildren to pay. So instead of getting out of the responsibility of raising their children like they thought they were getting, they just turned all the authority of the children over to the government. Now government owns the children which is all Mystery Babylon has wanted from the beginning. With the government for their only god, Mystery Babylon running our Government, the children came out getting the short end of the deal. Must be true for it seems that both, the parents and the government are well pleased but I don't see very many pleased children, or spiritually successful children, in character or physical material, not even in their own eyes. The ones that would qualify for Hillary's school could move into running the country, paid for by the taxpayers. And don't call a one of them, illegal aliens or terrorist, for it will offend them; they vote for the Democrats, and you will be prosecuted. Their attorney general telling us we would.

A very big plan, but not even the great Clintons could pull it off, yet! The Devil don't give up easy. God sets our rulers in office and it seems he had no plans to let them go that high. Even at the point of them, being at their highest, God threatened them both with their lives, by their health. I believe if it would have been necessary he would have taken either one or both out. God had another plain and had no intention of selling us down below a third world country, under the world's false gods, that easy.

If that was what we wanted he would just give it to us in a big complete way, and that is what he did. A Muslim that could not even prove he is a citizen of our country and seems nobody believed he would be elected. That should have showed anybody that God put him in there like he said he did.

God told me before the election he was going to do it, and wanted me to know it was his doings and not to get in his way. Obama went in, immediately announcing this was not a Christian Nation any more. I agreed with him on that one, for I could not see a Christian nation electing a Muslim. But when he said the country's worst enemy was the Christians holding onto their God and guns, and was the blame for all the world's problems. Using up the rest of the world's energy and oxygen, and he was going to put a stop to it. I disagreed fiercely with him on that lie, but the blame American, God haters, fell all over him, with his cutting off Christian's heads plan. His plan is to take the guns and the money from anybody that has any, unless they are supporting him with it. And cutting off our energy supply, and he was going to control it for us. And kill anybody in the world that would not accept Muslim over Christianity. This is his constitutional protected religion. While Christians receive the death penalty. This is a Democrat's interpretation of our constitution. I believe anybody that was not wearing a pair of Satan painted, rose colored glasses should have been able to have seen it. The Bible says that God haters are deaf and blind. I believe he proved it with that one.

You show me one who could not hear what Obama was saying all along and I'll show you one who is willingly deaf and blind that was determined to fall to such a God hating philosophy; and a lying Democrat Supporter. An Obama lover, with a reprobate mind as described in the Bible in the first chapter of the book to the Romans.

And the college smartened public lawyers, judges, teachers, preachers, theologians of all kinds; have no idea of what went wrong. Being educated by the Great Mystery Babylon Whore Church that is setting on the head of the seven-headed beast that the sixth head has gone into perdition, there at Rome. That has taken over our whole country and outlawing our Bible and Constitution. Like God said they would do.

I remember when I was just a very small boy; the mother of harlots and abominations church was telling us, if they could have a child until after his first three years of schooling, he would never believe another religion. I will mention other times when Satan warned us and we could not see it. Before I finish this book.

I believe they think it cannot be wrong for it is just what we all wanted. Even if they were the ones that sold it to us. Why should anyone dare suggest that it is wrong? It does take a little nerve, for you could end up in jail, and certainly losing a lot of friends, and maybe your head. I have decided that if I lost a friend over telling the truth. Then I am not the one that is losing in that transaction. I have dedicated my life to stating the truth so has everybody else that has accepted Jesus Christ, for he is truth and nothing else. It seems easy for a lot of people to forget that. I try hard to remember, and that is hard for the flesh to accept. Devil possessed people cannot accept it. God accepts no part of any lie, or our flesh.

When God told me before the first election of Obama that he was going to put Obama into the white house and for me to know it was his doings and to not get in his way. I did not fully understand. But I understood not to get in his way and I have not. I have gone right on preaching truth. Which is the Bible and what the spirit gives me, and I did not vote for Obama. I hope and intend for you to understand some truths if you read much of this book.

Remember the Bible is the Word that Jesus said all will be fulfilled before the end comes. We would be very wise to never forget it, and to never get in his way. Anything that gets in God's way of fulfilling his Word will be destroyed out of his way, saved or not. I've seen a lot of people get away with a lot because they just did not get in God's way. I've seen people taken out or down for small matters because they got in his way of him performing his word. God has a plan, if you want to get along with him and work for him you must study the Bible and get lined up with him. You will get nowhere in the Spirit without him, he is the Spirit. The Bible is spiritually written and discerned. The Spirit is the real thing, and is in authority over it all. The carnal is just an image of a spirit.

I believe, just this day God has given me some deep understanding as to what he is doing and why. The biggest question I had of all of them was why he put a Muslim in our white house controlling our laws and military and about everything else, even congress. You might want to find out what the number one religion in congress and this great country is. It would be a great help to getting the understanding of what I am going to try to explain and lay out here, before I finish. I believe if you will read it with any interest you will be knowing what the number one religion in this country is. Very controversial and may get on a few toes. Stay tuned if you can hang on, it will be Bible and the gospel truth or I will pay for lying. I suggest you check things out for yourself.

The Antichrist and False Prophet are two spirits very closely intertwined and using a lot of bodies to carry the same spirits. If you do not keep that in mind, reading about them, you can get them confused. Neither one is just a certain man but a spirit controlling certain men. Even many at a time, given a personal name. With God, a name denotes character. Whether a spirit or man. A man can only plan for himself only up to around seventy years, then he will be gone and must turn it all over to someone else. A spirit can work on a project up to a much longer time, seems like forever, but not so of course.

It makes one wonder why a man wants to get so involved, the challenge I guess, for his short time is a sure thing. Seeing his dedication and devotion you would not believe he knows that it is all toward himself. Man, is a puzzling machine, hard for God to figure him out, I think, but God knows him; and has revealed him to the world. The Word of God has revealed God to the world, to them that can read it with the Spirit of God's help. Reading it and handling it is two different things. Man, needs to seek God to have a correct understanding, of anything. Just the way God made things. -Then you can ask, If God is running everything, why is everything so messed up? Man, was given the Devil and the freedom to choose that side, if he preferred. Most of them chose the Devil, even being told and warned as to what he was, and where he would take us too. It is what they preferred. God has said, if you don't believe me, I do not want you. He will have a tried and proven people or no people, your chose.

CHAPTER 3

WHO IS AN ANTICHRIST?

How many ways are there to recognize an Antichrist? God tells us there are many of them. He said the flesh is at war with the Spirit of God, which is the Bible, Jesus Christ, and contains every God-given right to man, given by my Bible or Declaration of Independence or my Constitution. The flesh is antichrist.

God said to establish every word from the mouth of God with two or three witnesses from the Word of God. I believe that would be two or three witnesses, going both ways for each other. How do you think one could tear them apart and convince a Christian? You must ask a Mystery Babylon member, I guess, or a Democrat.

If someone tells me he votes Democrat, or is a college graduate, or is a successful lawyer or politician, and tells me he is a Christian; I will not fully believe him until I have seen some spiritual conformation. I know, I am not to judge any man, and don't, but God has also told me not to believe a lie. So, which way do you want me to go?

I will tell you big time which way I will go. I fully intend to go with my Bible in anything and everything. I try to run everything through my Bible before I move very far with about anything. If one can show me from my Bible where I am wrong, established from my Bible like it says, I want to be the first to want to make a change in the way I am going. Teaching anything contrary to the Bible is an Antichrist spirit, speaking blasphemy.

Anybody that puts a denomination or any other false god in front of my Bible, in my estimation, is an Antichrist. How can he be a Christian and have anything else setting in Christ's seat? Nothing but the Word of God can set there. The Word of God, Jesus, and the Father are one and I do not believe anything will ever change that. You must believe the Bible to be one with them. If not you are an Antichrist, I do not care how pretty a name you call yourself or how big a church house you have built for yourself. There is only one way, the Spirit of God.

With God, names denote character. If someone changes its character, God will change their name. The word Antichrist did not exist until the visions were showed and told to John by Jesus Christ. Look at the ones that have changed their names to Islam trying to copy our God. He said there is no other name under heaven by which men must be saved by. We have any amount of denominations telling us God has many names and he don't care what you call him, it is the same God. We are all children under one God. I believe they are liars and do not know the God I serve. Least that is what God has said.

You are free to call me a liar all you want to; I do not have a dog in that fight. I am a preacher of the Word of God and happen to believe it, and would not advise you to call it a liar even though God gave you every right to do so. He did promise consequences. We will face judgment for what we chose to believe. And believing a lie when we know better, will make you an Antichrist.

Jesus said if you are not gathering with him, you are scattering abroad. I do not read of any halfway house anywhere around God. I am sure there is people that could wrist the scriptures around and come up with one. But God said not to add one word to his word and not to take ought from any word in it. That does not give an antichrist much scriptures to play around with. If he does, it is no longer the Word of God, but his word and opinion. I would not think it would carry much power. Opinions are dead when the truth comes to light. And the Bible is the truth.

An antichrist might possess enough power in himself to put his fingers about your throat and choke you to death but it would not be the power from his scripture he perverted. If it was me, and I could find a big enough club, I might just quote the scripture God give us "There is a time to kill" and say this is it. I guess you could say it is all in the way of looking at it. I believe I could find many scriptures that would establish I can go a long way to protect me and mine. I have always saw and preached it that way.

This is another situation where I do not need someone that cannot read my Bible preaching to me what it means. They will have you believing you and God are the foolish ones. My God says it is them that are the foolish ones, and I am going to believe him. This is one of my points for this whole book. That antichrist's words have no power more than his own hands. God's Word applied can get his head cut off instead of mine, that his word tells him to do. God says a deceiver will fall into his own pit.

The Bible is written in a spiritual language as the Spirit gave it to the seventy or so, best English scholars that could be found in the country of England. Written in a low form of English language that the lowest man in England could understand it, when it was, *read to him*. Jesus, became the begotten Son of God when he was born into flesh from a seed of David. He grew into a man while learning by his sufferings. He was given all power on heaven and earth when he gave his crucified body back to the Father. Paying the sacrifice for all mankind that would volunteer to be reborn into the Spiritual Kingdom. Which was sent back by the Father and Son in the form of the Holy Ghost. All the world has been dating things from that time ever since. How can they deny knowing about him?

Jesus chose twelve of his disciples and trained them to preach the gospel to the world before he was taken from them. They evangelized over half the known world, before the Mystery Babylon Great Whore took over the church that Christ left at Jerusalem. By pretending to join it, and started control of it from Rome around the year three-hundred AD, by our calendar date. Their emperor burned all the paperwork he could find containing scripture. Made it a death penalty for anybody, but him and his, to be caught with a piece of scripture. I read they killed over a hundred million saints over the next few hundred years trying to stomp out any religion in the world beside their church's religion. This was the start of the Mystery Babylon Whore, Mother of Harlots and Abominations of the earth that John wrote so much about. Drunk on the blood of the saints and martyrs of Jesus. Riding upon the seven-headed beast with ten horns, and filled with the names of blasphemy. The antichrist ten kingdoms becoming the ten horns on the seventh head of the beast, in our time. Claiming to be the vicar of Christ here on earth. But does not believe in a Holy

Ghost Spirit, sent back by Jesus and God the Father. They are the False Prophet and an antichrist.

In around the year sixteen and eleven on our calendar, Jesus gave himself to mankind in the form of a book. Written in a Spiritual language that could be read and understood by man with the help of the Spirit of God. God made it plain, the carnal without the help from the Spirit, could not understand or receive anything from it. It was sought from God by the country of England because their country was in such disarray. Confused by so many denominations, books, and different doctrines of religion, each one claiming to be the right one. Just like America is today. God gave the right one to them in the English language with the agreement that it was his Son, Jesus Christ. Written by the Spirit of God, and they were not to add a word to it. Not another word and not even an English word that was added to the English language after, and certainly not from another carnal language on the earth, and not to take ought from a word in it. And to preach it to every other creature on this earth. That shut out all other carnal languages.

If someone tells you that it has been rewritten five times since the original or any such like thing, you can believe what you want to. But I checked into that deep, and you have my permission to tell him I said, "He does not know what he is talking about." And he probably does not know much about what anybody else is talking about either, along that subject.

Therefore, God does not need a word from them added to his Word. It is complete and perfect, and God has asked, "What can one add to the perfect?" There is nothing any more perfect and complete than God's Word. He put every word in it that he needed to say, and all that he wanted to say. We will need to keep on studying it, for we will not ever scratch more than the surface of the knowledge that is in it, in one lifetime. We could never remember it all if we did. If one does not seek God, he does not have him. Seek him, receive him, and just believe him is what God has said for us to do. You will be added *in* him, not *to* him. There is a difference. It is man that wants to add himself and all he can to God. Anybody that cannot believe that, is an antichrist.

I have heard some of the greatest teachers I know, use the Greek Bible to call Jesus a liar. Saying he did not know how to state the correct words when he wrote the King James Authorized translation. Which Christ said he wrote. I would be afraid to say that. I do not remember hearing him say he wrote the Greek or Hebrew Bible.

God has laid his arm bare to us, revealed his whole creation to us from the end to the beginning. Withheld no good thing from us and promised there would be no change in anything he promised to us. His Spirit will make it plain to them that have his Spirit, but we, being carnal, will not understand anything without his Spirit. This is man's problem; all flesh is carnal and can have no part with God. The flesh cannot have faith and trust in God, therefore it must die and the Spirit take over. The Spirit is the life in us, that are born again. God considered anything else, dead.

Sorry to be the one that must tell you, but any religion that does not believe in the baptism of the Spirit of God is a dead-to-God religion. By their confession, is the only way one can tell for sure if they have it are not. If they say they don't believe in it; my Bible says they do not have it. God has said to work to make our calling and election sure and be a witness for him.

How can we be a witness for him if we deny him? If you deny him down here, he will deny you before the Father. That will qualify you to be an antichrist. God says before the end of time; the whole world will take off after the Antichrist. Therefore, I stress the Bible so strong, it is the only thing that God says, engrafted, can save your soul.

One should know that God's Word does not get bogged down in unnecessary details about anything. I say there is not an unnecessary word in the Bible, and there is not one necessary word missing. If this is not so then you can just throw the whole Bible away, for it is a lie. But I would not know where to tell you to go to for salvation. Your favorite preacher, I guess, your choice should be just as good as the next man, don't you think? Just do not expect me to follow you and we can probably get along. For I know in whom I believe.

If the Bible got marred down into carnal details it would not be able to get out of the book of Genesis without being so big one could not carry it around. One could not get it read in one lifetime. I hope that is enough to get my point across, with a little thought. I explained it in my other books a little farther than that. John said, if all that should be wrote about Jesus was wrote, he reckoned the books of the world could not contain them. I say the Bible is maybe the most edited book in the world. It has everything any man needs to please God, if he will study, hear, and believe it.

The Bible makes plain, one is to seek and listen to someone that is anointed and sent by the Spirit of God, to be saved. This is on our part to know the spirit of what we are dealing with. You can never be saved if the Spirit is not drawing you. If you do not know the spirit of something, you just do not know it at all. You should follow someone you can trust to help you, and that alone will keep you busy studying and checking through the Bible. It is the only judging standard of everything in the world. If you get your eyes set upon a man, you are doomed to fail if that man is not Jesus Christ.

I was told years ago, by my father; "It will keep you busy at least half of your time, to mind your own business. It will keep you busy the other half of it, leaving the other man's business alone." I have remembered it for seventy years now and found it to be very worthwhile. I have taught hard we are to know what are business is.

I do not know any religion on this earth any more antichrist, by their own teaching and actions, than Islam and Muslim religion. John, gave them the very name, Antichrist, the only writer in the Bible to use that name. I do not know the difference in the Islam and Muslim religion, just that both are sworn to, and rewarding for, killing all Christians and Jews from the earth. And many so-called Christians teaching and trying to tell me that we are all God's children and serving the same God and have one Father. Somebody forgot to tell Jesus about it. He never taught no such thing. He told a good-sized denomination, the strictest of his time, that their Father was the Devil. I know a lot of people that do not believe Jesus Christ. I have told a few that they may be serving the same God that the antichrist is serving, but they are not serving the same God I am serving. Somebody is a bigger fool than God has said we were, being carnal.

This country's first wars were fought with Islam radical extremist, foreign and domestic. It is where our marines got one of their theme songs from, from the hills of Montezuma "To the shores of Tripoli."

We have been fighting them off since the first of our existence until now. King Richard, was England's hero for fighting them. Our schools are now teaching he was just a bigger fool than our fore-fathers were. He drove them out of Europe. I believe the Mother of Harlots and Abominations and the Moslems would not want to face another King Richard or any of our founding fathers again. Even though they are teaching our children, they were fools.

The war on Christianity has never been greater than it is right now. Seems like we have never had so few Christians that will stand up for a Christian. They have been duped by the Mother of Harlots and Abominations of the world church there at Rome. And are following the god, called, the False Prophet leading the mother church. We have fought two world wars against them, and won. They are now trying to team up with the Antichrist Kingdoms of the East to rule the world once again. And they will, for a very short time.

God says the ten kingdoms, ruled by the Antichrist himself, is going to give their power to the beast that the Mystery Babylon Whore, controlled by the False Profit, is riding. In the Bible language, saying giving their power to them, simple means they are merging in with them. But the antichrist kingdoms will eat the Babylon Whore's flesh and burn their city off the earth. They have started eating her flesh now. This is the so-called war on Christians that is going on now, over the world, but is hardly getting started. Mostly in the Middle East and the amount they can penetrate our country, which is an amazing amount today, and is increasing at an alarming pace. It would be better called a war on hypocrites, but some good Christians will get caught up in it. Even though God has warned them.

I have a bit of, sixteen-hundred to two thousand-year old news for them, if they care to hear it. John wrote it out very plain in his books of Revelations that Christ gave to him on the Island of Patmos. The False Prophet and the Antichrist Islam kingdoms are going to team up and make up the Mystery Babylon Beast Riding Whore that Jesus showed John and described to him in the wilderness. They will form the seventh head on the Roman beast and will rule the world, for a short time. The ten kingdoms will be the ten horns on the beast's seventh head. But the ten Antichrist kingdoms have not been broken to ride and God has put it into the hearts of the Eastern Kingdoms to hate the Whore. Vatican City, there at Rome, will be burned off the earth, then the Antichrist turns to finish off Israel. Christ has said, this is not going to happen. But the Jews must call out to Christ, in order-to be saved. This is what Christ has been waiting for, to set up his kingdom on this earth.

A few days ago, I heard a preacher, on the TV, trying to explain when Christ was going to come back, talking about a rapture. I told them, if he knew when the Jews were going to cry out, "Blessed is he that cometh in the name of the lord" then he would know exactly what time Jesus was going to come back again, but not until.

This country was founded and built upon the Bible, (Jesus Christ, which is the same thing). When it was held up front as our flag, we were exceptional and the leader, in about anything on the earth. Up through the first half of the twentieth-century; we did not know what it was like to lose a war. That is, only the Democrats losing the Civil war. We let the two Biblical, satanic powers that God warned us about all up through the Bible; the Antichrist and the False Prophet, move over us subtle just like God said they would. Taking control through the Satanic Democratic party controlled by the Mother Church from Rome; while we were sleeping or dead. Even though she was not named until John came along. I do not know which spirits, but Satan was their god for sure. John's writings, the book God was talking about when he told one of the prophets to quit writing; there would be another book wrote later that would cover the thunders that he saw.

Daniel only prayed to be shown what was to happen in the end to his people, the Jews, through the eyes of the Jews. John was showed what was to happen to the end of the Gentiles, down to God coming down from heaven, in new Jerusalem, to make his abode among men.

Daniel wrote nothing about the Antichrist or the False Prophet by name. John wrote about little else, past the forth chapter of Revelations. Jesus, did not become the written Word of God and given to mankind until around the year sixteen and eleven when England sought King James to come up with an Authorize Version of Scripture that would solve their religious problems of confusion and divisions they had there in England.

He did, the King James Authorized Version and God ordered them to preach it to every creature in the earth; and to the Hebrew and to the Greek. God has since blessed and protected any people that has taken it and held it up, even better than he said he would. But he will drop any people that drops it. He has said he would.

England first then America, they were both made into being the most blessed and powerful country up until their time. They have both went down at the same ratio and time as they have turned from the teaching of the Bible. There is nothing any plainer that can be found in their history.

Only a person in denial, could check and not see that. Even after Mystery Babylon rewriting on our history, for maybe sixty years.

When the pilgrims and the puritans were drove out of Europe, they took their Bible with them. It was a sacred book and they knew their very souls and spirits were depending upon them believing, trusting, and protecting it not only for their survival but their increase for generations to come, survival also. A bunch of faith and foresight embedded in them and the ones they raised.

God sent them an amazing bunch of men with an unbelievable

Amount of foresight, courage, faith, and determination. When Washington left the government that he and so many others had fought and built up and established. One of his stern pieces of advice was, they should never sign a binding treaty with the European countries, ever. Now the Mystery Babylon Whore, teaching our children that King Richard and our forefathers was some of the wickedest people ever was and got our noses into so many treaties that we cannot turn our head. They still cannot handle us after two world wars, and never will if we hang onto our Bible, which is Jesus Christ. So, they have taken total control of the country, and are fixing to get the ten, Antichrist Kingdoms, to join them in their conquest of the world. That will be their downfall but the rise of the Antichrist to rule the entire world with their help.

Remember when God broke up and scattered Babel by taking their language, saying if he did not, nothing would be restrained to mankind if they could remain as one. At the right time, he has sent us Jesus in the English language that has brought the world together like no other kind. The

Bible, our Declaration of Independence, the Constitution are in the English language. Look what the World has accomplished, space, everybody that is anybody can talk all over and send pictures all over the world through space. Explosives that they say could blow the world out of orbit. I am afraid to ask what they are going to come up with next. But I can assure you that Jesus still has things under control if we will receive him, no wonder he told us to fear him.

America is in a great conflict now, the worst it has ever faced. We have been taken over by the False Prophet Church there at Rome, very subtle, like God said they would do. They have come through our school system starting at the top going to the bottom and spread out until they have control of every organization in this country except the true Christian, and they are becoming extent at a frightening pace.

America does not know where our exceptionalism comes from, or where it went, and is denying it, but the False Prophet and Antichrist Spirits, very well know. They are each a spirit controlled by Satan, and sworn to set their seat in the north parts, and receive the worship of God's congregation. Worship, just means to give honor to, God has said all honor that he does not receive, goes to Satan. When we speak for Satan, he receives all that honor; when we speak against God, the same thing. Spirits desire to use our bodies, they have been defeated and cannot lay a finger on you physically. But can temp your carnal mind and take control of your entire body, if you allow it. All one must do is believe a lie to be dammed.

Man, is double minded. He can listen to and use his carnal mind or his spiritual mind. Satan and his spirits has access to our carnal minds to temp and persuade our flesh to obey them and follow him, to go against God's Spirit. But only with lies, for they cannot speak the truth. Which is the Bible and Jesus Christ. Our flesh and carnal mind must choose to die out to Satan, for he is a lie and sin, and barred from having any position in God's creation forever. So is our carnal minds, they are in the same world as Satan.

Satan can temp us for an allotted time, to prove us worthy or unworthy, for an eternity of bliss with Christ forever. If you cannot love truth you will fail and be rejected. Jesus knows if you cannot love him, or cannot love righteousness, you could never be happy with him; but miserable. All Satan has, to temp anyone with is a temporary good feeling to our lustful flesh, that is all pointed toward death for your body and a hell for your soul for eternity with him.

The spirits (Created sons of God) tend to be jealous and envious of mankind. We are created above them, and can become equal to his begotten son. Which took on a body form and suffered death for us. They do not have a body of their own. They do not have male and female, and not allowed to take on a helpmate, as one. So, they are very desirous to make one of our bodies a dwelling place, especially if they can take total control of it. I do not believe they can talk our language unless they can take control of someone or something's voice box. You can study that out for yourself.

We speak by sound or vibration, a spirit speaks the same language that the whole earth started out with, before God confused it from us; at the tower of Babel. All species had to work out their own way of communication. The carnal with a transmitter of sound and an ear for a receiver, the spirit transmits and receives with feelings. They do not communicate together with one another very well until today.

I have not studied enough to lay out much about the transportation of a spirit. But it sure seems like, time, space, distance, gravity, and what we call pain and many other things that we deal with, has no effect or means, to a spirit. Makes it kind of hard to describe its way of moving around. It leaves no smoke or racket, so I guess there is no friction involved. Not much information to start a study on, but I guess it would be a start.

Obama saying Christians and guns are the biggest enemy to the world, is not very far wrong. Just not very plain, our Bible accounts for both. You cannot be a Christian without believing the Bible, and it is the best weapon that is in the world. Why do you think Christ haters are scared to death of the very word, Bible? Devil possessed people know its power better than our so-called Christians do. And there is no difference in devil possessed and radicalized people. Look at them from any way you like.

True Christians are told to not make any communion with the Devil or his people. They do not understand the word peace, as the spirit uses it. Jesus said he did not come to bring peace, but division. But I keep forgetting, Christians seem to be the very last ones to read what Jesus said. Christ said the Bible was what tells us about him. How do they expect to get to know Christ if they do not know how to read it? I guess with what somebody else tells them. I do not know two different preachers from different denominations that will tell you the same things about Christ. Unless it is from the Bible and aligns with the Spirit of God it is useless, and wrong.

So, when somebody tells me about Christ, I like for him to be able to establish it with at least two or three witnesses from the Word of God. Jesus said he does not need the testimonial from man, he knows everything in a man. I believe he was referring to man trying to explain God's Word. If it does not come from God's Spiritual Word then it is just someone's opinion, one of the cheapest things in this world. Everybody you meet is trying to give some of his away. I have very few people that is afraid of my opinion and that is alright. I have found a few that *does* fear God's Word, that is alright too. God said he was looking for people that would tremble at his Word.

We have listened to False Teachers in this country until we have let the Antichrist, Devil possessed, zealots' outlaw our Bible and the word Christ to be spoken in public and have told us they have saved us from ourselves. Now what true Christian is going to believe that? I guess we are supposed to thank them Democrats for saving our lives so unselfishly, but I just do not feel like I am indebted to them. If I thought a Democrat could save anybody, I would thank them.

I read where George Washington said no man could rightly rule in this world without the Bible. Of course, it could cost you your head, if you tell them Mystery Babylon Democrats that. I've been threatened several times in different ways myself, at least two times with a shotgun. Some of them are not around anymore, thank God, but they did not have me worried when they were. God has delivered me out of it all, as Paul said. But our colleges are teaching our children that our founding forefathers were just a bunch of trouble making, whisky making, low life womanizing, drunks. I am far from being at ease with a bunch of noxious leftovers, claiming to be Christians, rewriting our American history for our children. They have been very successful in controlling the scriptures and killing anybody caught with any part of one in their possession, for well over a thousand-year period. Over a hundred million of them been killed.

Of course, we have been taught they are so much smarter than us and it is not Christian to disagree with a college professor that is politically correct. That will get you to being called a hypocrite and will send you to hell for sure; accordingly, to them. Might get you locked in jail, or killed, before we won two world wars against them and their killings. But we would not finish them off neither time. Now God is having to raise up ten antichrist kingdoms, to finishing the job for us. We have had a burnout for God, worse than Elijah. But God has plenty of reserved forces as he did in Elijah's time.

Like I have said I have a belly full of people preaching to me when they cannot even read my Bible, and do not know what it says when they do. And have killed over a hundred-million people for trying to read it. Politics has been running our country for forty to fifty years and look where it is at. I think it is overdue for a change, myself. And have been doing what I can toward one, but seems next too impossible for one man to make much difference. I can look at my close friends and family and easily see that it has made much difference. Even though they may be a small bunch. I thank God for them, from the bottom of my heart.

You can see how much the world leans toward people they seem to thank are so smart. This is another place where I pick up on my saying that carnal is always backwards to the Spirit of God. They see everything from the opposite side of the Spirit, and think God is the one that is backwards and upside down, instead of them. They will never get things right until they can get themselves straight. They are the ones that are wrong. God says the smarter a man thinks he is, the more foolish he becomes.

I like to give an example when I make a statement that I know blows so many out of the water. When Obama was first getting into the race for the Whitehouse; I had been keeping up with him a little; when one of them left-headed TV news-station's, anchor-ladies, was already campaigning for him, said, "He just might be the smartest man in the world!" I spent a minute picking myself up off the floor, thinking I would come nearer voting for him to be more on the other end of the scale stick. I have not improved my thinking about him after all these years of him being at the top of their pole. But this story helped me to nail down my belief, that if you do not see the spirit that a thing is of, you just do not see the thing at all.

God's opinion, which is always right, does not see the word *smart* like carnality sees it. He says the smarter we think we are the more foolish we become. God said knowledge is worrisome to the flesh. Remember how humans fell from God by eating from the tree of knowledge? It was not an apple tree, okay? It was a tree of knowledge and man cannot handle it very well at all. When the angel brought the knowledge to Daniel (And others) that he was praying for; he was sick for certain days and unable to do the kings business until he regained his strength. There is nobody any smarter than a man with common sense, and faith in God, and reads and believes the Bible. God is the author of common sense, which is his Word, the Bible.

Our colleges, thinking they are so smart, have worked around the clock trying to prove there is no such thing as common sense; or it is too much below them for them to recognize. You must turn it over to see it from the Spirit's side. That would put the common sense above them.

And the reason they cannot read the Bible, they have no common sense.

So, they have sent a man to the moon and a missile into space that has been traveling two-thousand miles an hour for several years and has not crashed into anything yet. Reckon it has gotten out of the shadow of God's little toe-nail yet? They do not have to worry about me, I am barely smart enough to get by. But I have a Spirit that dwells in me that is the giver of all knowledge, he says to fear him, and I do. I have that much common sense, but I hear a lot of smart people who don't. I think they may need to reset their compass. Where do they want to end up at?

I believe a compass is made to set a straight line in a certain direction. It is common for a lot of people to not know what direction they want to go in; why God has told us to wake up and get our minds straight. Our minds are to control our spirit; our spirit is to control our hearts. Our heart is what God looks at to judge us by. I say we are a mind thing, being operated by our minds, or our spirit. We are told to be very careful how we do anything. And be guided by the Word of God in everything.

CHAPTER 4

SPEAKING OF COMMON SENSE

I grew up on several years of working teams of mules and horses, in logging timber and farming and many other jobs, when I was very young. My dad was known as one of the best mule skinners that ever migrated from out of Kentucky. Even though, we did not always get along real smooth, I thought he was the best daddy that every migrated from Kentucky. I learned much from my dad about such things. When a team cannot learn to work together in about all ways; but works contrary to one another instead. You are not going to turn out very much production.

I see our government, trained by our college professors, trying to make this country work. Doing it so stupidly, that it is beyond belief. If you cannot read the Bible a little, you will probably not be able to hear a word I am writing. They are possessed by Satan and operating under the intention of destroying this country down to the last piece of bread or nickel. And don't like much having it done; by not having any common sense. They are trying to work a lie with a truth to pull a plow. That will never work. Then they are trying to get God to work as a team with Satan. That will not work. Then they try to get two lies to work as a team together, they will work, but a lie will only help and prop up another lie, nothing else. No way will it benefit the truth in any stretch of your imagination. Where has that gotten us? Where we are at, look around yourself.

When someone tries to work two truths together, Satan and his imps are whipping and disturbing the team until they cannot work together. Satan has over 80% of the world helping him. It is no trouble to see now, who is willing to work with truth, and who is determined to work for themselves. Now where is the progress going to come from to lead this country toward anything sound, like the truth? I pray you can open your spiritual eyes (A bird's eye view, overall) and look a while at what was just said.

I have great faith in Donald Trump, he has talked the very message of God and common sense from day one. He is set and determined to do right by this country and everybody in it if they are for America and God. Even if he must do it by himself. He is that kind of person, and that is the kind of person I'm praying for. What else can you ask of him? To try to please everybody? We know the devil possessed people will be tearing at him with everything they can pull lose, all the way. He did not want a teammate to work equal beside him until he attains the nomination, I can understand why. Who could he trust that Satan could not use against him? There is no such thing as that perfect a man. I feel sorry sometimes, for them TV reporters struggling so hard to put a spin on every word to make Hillary look better, while trying to make trump look like a heel. Must be a hard job, especially when their job and paycheck is hanging in the balance. It was a plow only one mule could pull. Donald Trump was that mule, and he is pulling it.

I predicted he could win when he first announced. I told my son, setting beside me, all the things that he would have threw at him; which was basically everything, from everybody. But I didn't believe they would be able to knock him out, for I said, he is not a man that is accustom to losing. And he is talking truth, that is the message of God. If he can just stick with it he is bound to win, even if the country is determined to stick with a lie and go completely under. He won the nomination, but God has told me plain, the presidency is teetering in the balance, it remains up to the country. If they do not wake up God has said, he will put Hillary in there. He has used the farthest we had in each direction, now it is left up to us to choose. It is starting to look awfully shaky to me now. I find it hard to believe how Devil possessed this country is. God has exposed Hillary from every side, and they are still hypnotized by her.

Now Bill Clinton is out there telling us, Trump is the biggest lair every. The one that is accusing, God says is Guilty of the same. God is smart; I have learned to trust him. Just in case you are accusing me here, I am not accusing. Just stating a fact, there is a difference. In case it isn't so, then I am lying. I do not know of anyone that could start to prove me wrong.

If Trump is elected, every big shot, on both sides of the established isle, knows they would be losing their power and sugar tits of trillions of dollars that they have gotten so used to. News media and school teachers included. Why would they want to watch that slide down the drain without a fight? That should be simple enough for anybody to see and answer. They were even willing to settle for Ted Cruse rather than Trump. That was bending real low for them. They knew what was coming if they got Trump. Letting on like he was too unpredictable and careless, was just some more of their lies. Even they, are not that stupid, but think we are. And a lot of us are, we've been buying their BS for years now. It is not a lack of common sense as much as it is just not willing to admit that they are low enough to understand common sense. I would rather think they are just not that high. I already said how they think and speak backwards. Thinking with Satan, against truth.

I just got back from visiting my little birthplace community I did some of my growing up in, not far from here. It is well settled in relatives and judgmental, self-righteous, successful, tithes paying church people. But one of the more solidified nest of old hard core Southern Democrats that I know of. I had a little trouble getting out of school in that area. I did not find much that we could agree on and don't have any more until today. And that was in the late forties and early nineteen-fifties. I call the beginning of our famous antichrist teaching; it was the first I saw of it anyway.

It started in our little one room school house when they started requiring our teachers to go to college through the summer, to acquire qualifications to teach through the winter; government orders. Our teacher came back with so much new information, she was hardly recognizable. It was not about math and science, but was more about a religion, called politics, and has not improved since. They had to outlaw the teaching of anything religious, so they could teach theirs. They would not call it religion, not even when it was coming from the Koran. Or from the Babylon Whore Church at Rome.

I'll never forget one of her first announcements at the beginning of the first day of school in around the year nineteen fifty-one. It happened during the big national school consolidation that I can never forget. She told us with glee, "I have learned so many amazing new things to share with you. Why! they have proven the world has not stood for just six thousand years, like we have always been told. But has stood much longer; maybe as much as *fifty thousand years*."

So right there around ten or eleven years old, went my Bible out the window. And as far as the government is concerned they have been standing at the window with a baseball bat to see that it never gets back in.

What did they do in the late forties and early fifties that proved that God had to create a baby earth with everything starting at zero? We count Adam and Eve to have been created around the age of thirty years. I have no proof, but saw no reason to dispute it. I do not read anything about them changing one another's diaper. I've learned I do not have to have proof to believe the Bible. Everything you can see, is its proof.

Could not God have called for a million-year-old earth just as easy as he could have called for a baby earth? What would he have had to done different that would have convinced the people of today at what time he created it?

Maybe he built a four-billion-year old earth and run the crank forward for three and one half billion and two years. Sat there and watched it for almost another one half billion years and then started time as we know it. Before he even built man or animals out of it. Like he said he did. He never said he played with time that much, only that he made man and animals out of the earth, and gave us a fair description of the time.

The Bible says with God one day can be as a thousand years or a thousand years can be as a day. Where can man prove one thing about time and age in his creation? Whose measuring stick are they going to use, man or God's? Or somebody else's that God hasn't showed us yet. What are we going to prove? God has time in his hands, and maybe fifty, or a million, hands, if he needs them. He can see it backwards or forwards, sideways or upside down and all of it at once. The only thing we can depend on is what he told us. Therefore, the Bible is so important. It is all we have.

Their problem is they cannot believe God created the earth, or anything else he said. They cannot create a God that can prove, or can even show, us if he did or didn't. One thing is for sure, God either created man or man created God. That is common sense. Which one do you choose?

It is all standing out there on nothing, how are they going to explain it, or deny it? If he slapped them across the face, a carnal mind cannot believe God created it. Even if he says he does, because a carnal mind is deaf and cannot hear, blind and cannot see, and void of any understanding; when he is confronted with the spirit, which is life. The Spirit of God is the only one that has any of that. Read what Jesus said, there comes a time with man when he doesn't need man to teach him anymore. If we are born again we are taught by the Holy Ghost. The Bible says so.

Listen to our educated men, how smart they have become, teaching each other. They don't even know their source to obtain knowledge from. If they don't know God, all they know is what somebody else told or showed them, and in a few years, he has forgotten everything he has learned. The Bible says there is no knowledge or work in the grave.

Then his son can start at zero and go through the whole process that his father attained and if he does not believe

God, will probably die with less knowledge and more lies than his father attained. Mostly lies of hopes and dreams, and all he will attain of them he will die and leave for somebody else. There went another generation. Been that way since somebody built the Egyptian Tombs, even before. Why and how did they do that?

How much deceit, lies and hate for the Lord Jesus Christ can our so-called Christians embrace and love, and still call themselves Christians? Maybe somebody should look up the word "Christian" in the dictionary and examine themselves a little, God says to. The word "Christian" is a spiritual word, and its definition can be found in the Bible, if you can find time to look.

People in this world are awfully busy. I do not know what the most of them are doing; I don't believe most of them do either. So, I do not feel all that more the dumber.

Just a few questions I would love to hear some Christians answer for me, but I would hardly know who to ask. If they will not volunteer, I would feel like I would be asking the wrong people. Of course, our parents think they are so smart and taught us it is not politicly correct to disagree with a college professor. He does control what you receive for a grade.

Politics is running our country now and it is against political laws to bring a Bible on school property. A very dangerous book to expose to any college age kid. One federal judge in Texas, threatened a high school graduating boy with jail time if he mentioned the name Jesus Christ at his graduation. I will not admit this is a lack of faith on our countries part; it is more on voluntary stupidity. And a big percent of the people in this country are Devil possessed. God said it was from being turned over to a reprobate mind because we do not love truth. One of the many ways and reasons, God has said he will destroy people that will not love truth.

I happen to be one that believes God, even though it has not gained me many friends. God is big enough to amount to more than all my friends. That does not mean I do not appreciate my friends, I do. But if I must give up my friends or my God, it will be my friends. God told me forty years ago, when I accepted him; "If I could not make up my mind to stay with him when it seemed like I was the only one. I would probably not make it." After forty years, I believe I have learned what he meant.

God is not cruel but is very plain if you have talked to him, you should know that. Far too many of us have never heard from him. Don't let that make you feel left out, for it takes time and effort to hear the Spirit of God and know him. We hear a carnal voice with our ears, but you will hear a Spirit with your feelings and very seldom will it be instantly.

Unless it is a wrong spirit, it will never be wrong. Sometimes we must test the waters a little, but if you will work at it and seek God you can continuously improve upon it. God will not give up on you if you will just stay with him. I have never heard him stick his head out of a cloud and yell at anyone. I'm sure there has been times he has felt like it. The big problem is, with us receiving his Spirit. Just remember you do not have to have someone else's approval, even if they think you do.

I believe every time I have heard a spirit in a carnal language he has used someone else's voice box, or believed the Bible. Might give that some thought. If we believe, seek, and obey God, the Bible gives us all we need to know, at least all we can handle. We do not have the capacity to hold but a very little of what God knows. He knows everything, and we are not able to handle any of it without God's help.

Therefore, we must learn to trust him. Everything is him, for he is everything, and everything he says is true. We could not move without him, if he just takes his breath back from us we will go back to the dust of the earth. To be burned up with the earth and the elements thereof which includes our earthy bodies. Now, can't you call God the biggest?

Our flesh is operated by our senses; we are created with having five I believe; our spirit is made up with the sum of our senses. When our spirit is gone, the bodies have no more senses. I do not know in what order they must leave in.

God has said, in at least two places I know of, "The inhabitants of the earth are nothing to him" and at least one place he said less than nothing. Every carnal thing on this earth is made up out of the elements of the earth and is false, temporary, deceiving and fake; an image; not the real thing. But the spirit is given of God, and cannot be seen or handled by man, only as he allows.

He gives each person a small spirit, tells us to align it with the Spirit of God or everything he has will perish and the spirit he has will go back to God. His soul will spend eternity with the spirit he chooses. Now you should be able to see why so much responsibility is put on the parents of children. Their very souls are in their hands. He said to *train* them in the fear and admonition of the Lord and when they grow older they would not turn from it. He said to train them, not order them. We all are to come to God as a child.

When he comes back and redeems his few that are ready to go with him, which is completely a spiritual thing.

He will burn up this entire creation and everything in it. Everything you can see on this earth is all material, physical, carnal and apart from the Spirit. Is not that about the same thing as mechanical or handmade? Our bodies are much the same thing, made and operated by the hand of God. Flesh is made from the ground, so is trees, steel and gold. Remember the first iron lung, that done the breathing for a brain-dead body, so to speak. It was very famous, covering half a room, incased a body laying down with the head hanging out. I believe, breathing for the person.

Now they have about the same thing, even better, hanging on a pole with rollers that a little 90 lb. nurse can carry in one hand. Along with mechanical hearts, arms, legs and ears. Boy, haven't we come a long way? Guess we have, considering it took God, they say, maybe billions of years to build a dog. I'm sure man thinks he has passed God up. Of course, God didn't have a computer. *sic.* Man, can build a robot, but it is defiantly another story to put life into it. Does he not know God could have made us into a world full of robots if he chose? But instead give us choses and a free will; hoping we would choose to serve him in righteousness. I feel grateful to God for the opportunity.

Man, still has-to look to the Son, or the Sun for life, in anything. One is for the spirit, and one for the carnal. The carnal is temporary; the Spirit of God is eternal.

One of his last promises he made to us when he left was, "Behold I make all things new," speaking of his return. He will burn the earth and the elements thereof that is made up of what we call substance or material matter. I'm sure it will include the computers; I do not see a spirit needing one. We have no evidence of spirits having any material about them, not even a body.

The spirit sounds weird to the carnal. Don't that mean that the carnal probably seems very weird to the spirit world? I believe if you look in the Bible real close you can see jalousie of God's born bodies in some of the angels. God could not allow unholy people into heaven after kicking out the created beings that rebelled which does not even need any space to occupy whether resting and doing nothing, or building a world. Space was made to create and store matter or material substance in and Gravity to hold it down to the earth, or a bigger body. God spoke to me just a short time ago and said, "Space can only be measured by time." I am still studying on that one. Our spirits that have been rebellious to God in this life will go back to God and will undoubtable be cast out with the spirits of Satan which, turned loose will be much more powerful than any of us. I've never heard of a spirit having blood, or pain, or a need for gravity, but can be much tortured.

Lucifer, the Antichrist, the False Prophets, the three fallen spirits that John saw like frogs, coming out of the mouth of the dragon beast, there in the book of revelations, were part of the wrath of God being poured out on the earth. The three spirits and all their imps will be filled with vengeance against God's born again people. For us in the carnal, to become Spiritual beings is to become a new creature, but to the spirit world the carnal is the new creature now. Just depending on which way, you are looking at it from. The carnal sees from one direction, the spirit sees from the other direction. The carnal and all fallen spirits are from behind looking forward or from the bottom looking up. The Spirit of God is just the opposite, up and forward looking down and back at us. Right now, we are sort of caught in the middle.

Why I say, everything is what it is, as to the way you are looking at it from. The Bible says, God declared the end from the beginning. Does not that mean to us he was at the end when he declared the beginning? He is still at the end, or top, looking at us to make it to him. If we give up, we will not make it to him. He sees everything from the opposite side from us. That makes us seeing things backwards from the Spirit. Every watch traffic in a rear-view mirror, or a TV from a mirror? John Wayne draws his pistol with his left hand and mounts his horse from the right side. An image reflects something, we are an image of the spiritual and shows up backwards to the carnal, we just need to realize there is a difference in seeing things from the carnal and seeing things from the spiritual.

They are from the opposite sides; you must make a few adjustments. Of course, the Spirit sees things clear through, but I would not know much about that. But I have just read that described in my Bible, maybe I will write on it when I get it studied out a little.

Like a truck driver considering his mirror, things can look larger or smaller, closer or farther and their right side will look like their left, takes some getting used to.

The carnal is an *image* of the real thing, not the real thing itself, even though it wants to believe it is the real thing and the spirit is the image. But that is just wrong. We cannot even go without the Spirit and when we think we are going without God, we are headed toward self-destruction, guaranteed.

The people who think they are succeeding in what they want to do without God, would probably faint if they just knew all the ways God was using them. To punish his people, to help his people, to turn his people, to wake them up, to open their eyes. To support his people, and to help them maybe see a better way to go; by using the heathen as an example. If they cannot wake up and learn they will reap just like the heathen. God says he works everything to the good of them that love him. He didn't say he uses everything to the good of all them that he loves, he scourges and chastises them, and cleans them up. Even that is for their own good.

He says he loves them that love his son. Read your Bible. If you find where he says he chastises and cleans up the devil's people, I pray you will show it to me. God said he would sacrifice the heathen for his people. And don't give me that carnal line, that we are all God's children. Jesus told some they were the children of the Devil. Do you think Jesus lied to them? I don't believe I would say that. Anything carnal has chosen the Devil for a father, or as Paul called them that denies the Devil, a bastard.

You study long and hard enough and look hard and long enough, you will be able to see what I'm saying about flesh being backwards, and cannot be a child of God. And how everything is what it is per where you are looking at it from. How come we cannot teach our own children a little truth instead of a barrage of government lies? We are ordered to see it like the government sees it. Flesh is warring with the Spirit; they are contrary one to the other.

As I've said in all my other writings, God pretty much made everything in twos. Any difference in things is one being closer to one side and farther from the other than the other thing that is different. Like closer to the front end and farther from the tail end, or closer to the top and farther from the bottom, and everything has its place and will be put there at the end. I have never seen a coin that didn't have two sides, or a stick that didn't have two ends, unless it was made in a circle coming around with both ends meeting. And you can go around and around on it without finding an end. But you are going nowhere but around and around and getting nowhere. And I have heard very few circles being called a stick.

The Spirit of God is always going up and forward, owning to if you are seeing parallel or horizontal, it is always moving. Anything that is not moving seems to develop dead spots, and living things die in them if trapped. Everything of the Spirit is always moving. I am not so sure about the spirit moving, but everything in it is. Even the bottom of the sea is being moved by the wind and moon and storms. They tell me the molecules in steel are being moved by magnets, heat and with a hammer. The earth is moving around and around at the equator which is twenty-six-thousand miles around. If it makes one revolution in twenty-four hours, that calculates over a thousand miles an hour.

The Bible tells us very little about the top not even its location, just that it is up. Up is not a place, it is a direction. We do not know how high up is. And don't seem to be getting closer to finding out. We know that the bottom is down, called the pits of hell and at least one of them does not have a bottom to it. The place was made for the Devil and his angels and them that will not have the Spirit of God. They will go there as unwanted guest and will be tortured with much misery for eternity. How long do you reckon it will take for man to find something that God has not told us about? Man, has not found it yet.

All this time he knows somewhere between nothing and very little about what is in the center of the earth, the bottom end. He has gone farther but knows very little more about what is out in space, the top end, than what he knows about what is in the center of the earth. Hell, is down and bottomless, does not the center of the earth qualify for that. Think about it, any direction you look or go opposite from down is up. You cannot go down any farther than the center of the earth unless you go up first, and any direction you look from there, is up. Then back down only just as far as you went up. Don't ware yourself out.

I do not believe man is progressing nearly as far and fast as he thinks he is. I'm still looking for man to be able to calm a hurricane, Jesus did. And some say that Jesus cannot do the things he said he did, and they say they can prove it. I heard Bill O'Reilly and Goldburg both call Jesus a liar. Saying they could prove it. That would be interesting to watch, almost as much as it would be to watch Jesus do them.

Man, can sure come up with some big interesting ideas and statements about what he can do, and how much he knows. When Jesus says, he can do nothing without him. Wonder which one knows what he is talking about, God says he can do more than we can imagine. Ever watch Star Wars and Star Trek? God can make them look like child's play, maybe that is what they are.

My first two books talked some bit about things being made in twos, with two sides and two ends. Language being one of the more vital things to accomplish unity in anything. Division being the opposite of unity. How Jesus came to bring division not peace. How he divided the people that was becoming one, against God. How Satan is a copier and has no creative power of his own, but has no other assignment but to kill, steal, and destroy. Division has become one of his favorite words. The creation had fallen to

Satan, except Able; Satan had him killed. God started over again with another son from Eve, Seth. With Cain being set free, the world was sentenced to kill off one another or leave vengeance to God. They had been given the whole earth as a garden to till for their living. They were to learn to trust God for settling their problems, by casting out the unruly people.

But they chose to settle their own problems, and leave God out. That was not a very smart decision, it left vengeance up to man to even his own score with everybody else. Every time one man thought he evened up a score, another man (Or two or three) thought he caused another score for them to have to settle. Ever hear about the Hatfield's and the McCoy's? Which one of them was in the right?

Reckon anybody ever figured all of that out? So, there is no way God could ever turn vengeance over to man. God is not unfair, just a lot smarter than man; and wants us to trust judgment over to him.

When Jesus said, he came not to bring peace, but division, he was completely talking about separating the world's people that had rebelled against God from among his people that would receive him. They were given the rest of the earth if they would stay out of the way of God's people. But God's people joined all the earth in being organized against God. A project he has been working on since the garden. He has not changed, maybe changed his methods a little along, but with more help for his people with every new covenant. Read your Bible it is explained all through it.

The Devil being a copier has tried to do everything to God's people just like God has done to his. We are willing to listen to him as our father rather than listen to God, our real father. Jesus came to save us with truth and them that will not love it cannot be saved. They speak two different languages, as I have written in other places. Jesus is nothing but truth, the Devil is nothing but lies. And trying to divide God's people any way he can, even trying to divide one word in half, down to kill and destroy it. Every word can be divided into a carnal meaning or a Spiritual meaning. Two languages I have been writing about. Take the word LOVE for example. God said he is love, but he has listed a dozen or so things that he does hate. Do you reckon he is mixed up and does not know the difference in the two? Satan would love that. But I am not very interested in Satan's definitions.

The first thing that anyone must accept, if he is to receive anything from the Word of God. God is not the one that is confused. Even though it is plain that somebody is. It will never be God. Do you remember me just saying that God and Christ is nothing but truth, and this Word of God is Jesus Christ, and they are one? If you cannot accept that, then you do not have any need to read the Word of God until you can. Therefore, God said the carnal cannot have this Spirit, it talks a different language. I dislike having to put it that plain, but it is the truth. Would you prefer me to lie to you about it so you would like it better? I am not in that business. I hope and pray that I never will be.

What the Devil calls love and has taught us to believe; is what God calls lust. Try it out, switch the words around in accordance to where they are coming from. You do not have to take my word for it. That would be good on your part if you didn't. You can read what I just said by looking the two words up in the Webster's dictionary, they are not far apart nor hard to find, love and lust. I am writing these facts and examples because I am literally sick of watching the TV's liberal talking-experts, and the ones that are listening to them. Using Satan's tactics to sell lies to a gullible country of people because they sound so satisfying to their lust. Lies lead nowhere but down into the pit, with everything that is attached to them.

Glenn Beck, a man I once used to just about worship for around three years. Watched and spoke out for him about more than anybody, but now have about quit him. I am a little bent on prophesizing but have been amazingly correct, that sometimes it frightens me a little. I told my wife some months ago, that Glenn was getting himself ahead of God in his lecturing and if he didn't get himself back on the sound truth, he was in danger of losing his TV station that God had handed him. I think he has just about fell out of his spiritual tree. Just for preaching one side of a word and doing the other side of it. Love is just one of them. He changed his whole TV station to attacking Trump, if he would keep his facts straight and solid I could stay with him, but he doesn't. He preaches love and forgiveness as being the only way, and makes mountains out of mole hills about ten and twenty-year-old things he accuses trump of being guilty of. All of them as far as I know, with no conviction at all, or not even close to one. I take it because he is so wrapped up in Ted Cruse, and he has about sunk Cruse, them being among the biggest dividers in the Republican party. Remember I said Satan has made, *division,* his business, trying to copy Jesus. He has also made, *accusing,* his business. I do not see Glenn and Ted preaching any more about righteousness than Trump. But very busy at accusing, God says that he that accuses is guilty of the same things (Romans: two). I have found no scripture any truer than that one. I've been studying it for years.

He preaches a half day on the fact that no one knows what Trump will do. He is so unpredictable and dangerous. Then preaches the other half of the day telling what Trump will do. Is he a spiritual seer or something? I say if Trump was so simple, weak, and flimsy that Beck could sat up there and read him off for the next eight years. I do not believe I would want to vote for him either. That is nothing more than a copy of Democrat strategy; that I am sick of. I give Trump much more credit than that.

Glenn talks about how Trump is not capable of leading this country, then tells about how he will lead it into destruction. Can he lead it are not? Seems somebody is a little mixed up. I'm not trying to attack Beck, I am still mighty high on most of him, just believe he slipped off the track a little, I hope it is temporary, and he will get back to truth. That is what Christians are about. I have noticed that when someone gets off track after being so solidly on it, they seldom get back completely. They have a hard time living with the guilt, I reckon.

I am just trying to point out, as I said, something that I see all over my TV, and must hear from the people that are listening to them. When it is so contradictory and talking out of both sides of their mouths, and covering the world. That it is starting to make me sick. As it is getting to be bigger all the time. That is my opinion and as everybody says, I reckon I am entitled to it.

I mentioned language again, it is hard to stay away from. God gave the Spiritual language of Jesus Christ, to the English people in the English language, because they sought him for it and agreed to his orders that come along with it. Anybody else that receives it must do the same thing. We did not have Jesus in that book form or language until around the sixteenth century. They were told to not change a word in it and to preach it to every creature, and preach it to the Hebrew and the Greek also. He did not say they already have a Bible; you don't have to share yours with them. That is not what God said. I have not read where he said to get our Bible approved by the Greek and Hebrew Bible, or where he told the Greek or Hebrew to preach their Bible to the English people.

I learned early in my preaching and Bible studying; sometimes it is just about as important as what he didn't say, as what he said. God said not to add to his word, before he said not to extract from it.

It has not been changed and never will be. They have been trying to rewrite it in a carnal language ever since God gave it to us but they can never do it. They cannot correctly call it an Authorized King James Translation if they change one word in it. They may be messing with God if they try to. A carnal language is an antichrist language, filled with carnal reasoning. God does not want a carnal word mixed into any of his Word, and said so. If God did not say a word, then he did not say it. If he said it, he meant it.

God said that in the last days the whole world would take after the Antichrist, it is looking like we are almost there. As I have said a few times, politicians can have my head cut off but it will not change one word in that Authorized King James Translated Bible. Try to count them that has been murdered all up through the Biblical times and God has not changed one word in his Word and never will. If you are one of the billions that will not believe his Word, you will not be moving into eternity with him but will be cast into the lake of fire at the end of the last battle. That was prepared for Satan and his angels. This is what God has said. It is not going to change. If you cannot believe the Authorized King James Translation that he said he wrote, you might as well throw it away and try to find your way around by feeling around in the dark.

Speaking of words and not getting them out where they can be properly received. I just received a dream about a word that I may need to try to explain a little farther in depth that I have used a lot. I will try to not mess it up farther.

The much writing, I have written about, two or many, becoming *one* in the spirit and can only do that in the spirit. Some material things can be mixed together into one, but the contents will be doubled unless some has been done away with. In other words, they can still be measured; but we have no way of measuring a spirit from the carnal. There is no evidence I know of that we lose our identity or individuality, to anyone but the one we are one with, not to all the others that are one with him. I cannot understand me knowing everything that all the others know or have all the same things they can have and do. But I believe that Jesus can know all the things about all of us. I do not believe we can know everything he knows. I guess we will just have to wait and see how some things is going to work out. Just some food for thought, I do not want to be taken as talking above my head; trying to keep me down to things I can show us. I can only go by what the Bible says or shows us by example; when it comes to a spirit.

The Bible says we will know as we are known, it seems that leaves some bit of space; as to how much we will know. I do not have a problem with it, just cannot explain it completely or real clear. I trust God and am sure he can handle it and I will not get cheated.

CHAPTER 5

CARNAL WORDS AND SPIRITUAL WORDS

I write a lot about languages, and how important they are. You cannot seem to have an organization or unity in anything without language unity. The carnal and the spiritual are looking at anything and everything from different directions. Your left side is entirely on the opposite side from your right side. So, it is, in physical or spiritual, but you are talking about two different things. The left side in spiritual is a complete different thing than the physical. One is talking of material things, while the other is talking of principals, and psychic matter, such as morality, decency, a whole new ball park.

Take the word, *good,* for an example, it is a Biblical word used much by Christ. God did not think it good to try to mind someone else's business, while the hippies developed a slogan that said, "If it feels good, do it." Don't you believe there is a little conflict between the two on the meaning of the word good and how it is accepted?

In the Democrat administrations, they talk of, *piece,* about more than almost any other word, while incorrectly preaching to us Christians that it is our most commanded thing. Do they think Moses, Joshua and Saul was preaching peace and love when they were told to go into some of the other people's land and kill everything that breathed; old people, women and children, even their cattle? Jesus himself said he did not come to bring piece but division. When he talks of his peace, it is not as the peace that the world gives. He said so. That brings up the word, *kill,* that has much room for some study. I will hit on it a little later. The Bible says to establish every word that comes out of the mouth of God, with other scriptures, and tells how to do it. These things, are why I am very full of, and strong on, just facts. I do not need a carnal minded college trained preacher to preach my Bible to me in any way. It is spiritually written and discerned. Why can they not read that?

The three evil spirits that John saw and wrote about and personalized, in his writings of the Revelations, Jesus gave to him. Coming out of the mouth of the dragon, the beast, and out of the False Prophet as frogs. These are the same three spirits that Christ throws into the lake of fire in and after the battle of Armageddon, along with every soul whose name is not written in the Lamb's book of life; and are members of Mystery Babylon.

These three evil spirits named and described in the last seven chapters of the book of Revelations are; the dragon (Satan) the Antichrist (the ten kingdoms of Islam) the False Prophet (the Mystery Babylon Whore Church, rider of the seven-headed beast there at Rome). They will all be thrown into the lake of fire, during and after the battle of

Armageddon. The Antichrist and the False Prophet before, the last battle. The Dragon is after.

Only then will the old heaven and earth be done away with, and the new heaven and earth will appear, coming down from heaven; for God to set his dwelling place up among men.

I have heard preachers trying to explain what the new things that Christ is going to send down is going to look like to us. I don't mean to be criticizing anybody, but God says this is impossible for us to do. Things spiritual are not seen and heard by the carnal eyes and ears, and the carnal cannot understand them. They do not know one thing more than the word of God tells us. It says they will be new things and will not be like anything we know about. Jesus Christ is the Word of God, and the same as the life we have in us. Can you tell what it looks like? A zombie is a person with no Word of God in him, God considers them dead. I am just trying to make plain the two languages used by the spirit and the carnal. They do not mingle together with the same definitions. People that cannot read a spiritual language cannot read the Bible with any understanding. Therefore, God says plainly, the carnal cannot receive anything of the Spirit. And has said that a preacher, to preach the Word of God, must be sent by the Spirit of God. That makes a carnally minded person mad to tell him that, but I cannot help that. It is what the Bible says and teaches. He will just have to get over it. If he wants to be saved.

I have written in other places; the Bible has its own built in dictionary. If you wish to put life in yourself, study your Bible. The King James Authorized Translation was not given to man until around the year sixteen-hundred. It is spiritually written, the Spirit of God itself claims to be the author of it. While Christ claims it to be him in person, in word form. I believe they have confirmed them both to be correct. It is the Spirit of God and the life of anyone that can believe it. It is the food for a spiritual man.

Even the carnal mind that is dead to God should be able to see why the world and man government all hate it. It reveals they are all dead and want to kill, steal, and destroy any person that has any life in them. The Spirit of God is our only protection. The Spirit of God; the Word of God; Jesus Christ; they are all one and the same thing. Therefore, God says we must walk in them. The carnal cannot see or believe any such thing. It can only be received by faith, that leaves out the flesh.

Any denomination that does not believe in the baptism in the Holy Ghost is dead to God, and has only the protection it can provide for itself. This, is why, we have so many churches with no spiritual power. They are Spiritually dead. That does not mean that everybody in it is dead, but the denomination is dead. Each one is to be in the Spirit of the Lord Jesus Christ.

This is not my doctoring; it is what the Bible teaches. They will find nothing to gain by finding fault in me or anybody else. They have the assurance that God will judge whether I am telling the truth. You can know, if you will study your Bible. I would suggest you do, before calling me a liar, just for your own safety. God is going to judge all of us. If you find me to be wrong, and establish it by the Bible, I will greatly appreciate it if you will show me. If we can improve our teaching, we will greatly improve our generation. Might even save our country from complete annihilation, but we know its dominion is gone, Daniel told us that. But if we would wake up and unite we could easily maintain our own dominion. What would be wrong with that?

The dictionary gives the definition of the word generation as "That being generated." Can we not see that what we are teaching and raising our children to be is what we are generating? They will be the next generation. It will be called our generation. Where is, Christianity going to fit into it all, when it has been taught and ordered out of our society completely? Who gave them Mystery Babylon Democrats, from Rome, that kind of authority? I will answer that, we so called God's people have. As we have said, carnal and spirit does not mix well, at all. If we do not know things by the Spirit they are of, and the spirit we are of, how do we know the difference in them, or which one is which, or who is who?

I wish to tell you something God showed me through several visions, after getting grieved in my spirit and much searching them through the scriptures with much prayer. God started into revealing to me many small things, very plain. One of them was, there can be much torture and much misery in the spirit without pain as we know it. Have you ever read where anybody inflicted pain upon a spirit? Not even when Jacob hung onto the angel until dawn and would not let him go. Even though the angel touched Jacob's thigh and crippled him for life. We know the angel must have been suffering torture and misery for he begged to be let go saying he had to get out of there. It was coming daylight. But no indication of any pain our damage was even being threatened to him.

Pain may very well be one of the best friends given to the flesh. The flesh is so limited to seeing (And many other senses) that it can only see in one direction at a time.

And then a certain amount like a shotgun vision, has no ability to see all around at once; has much difficulty seeing through matter or around a corner. I believe that would be strange to a spirit if he could not see every direction all the time. Have you ever read, very much even in carnal writing, where somebody slipped up on a ghost? Ghost is just an old English word meaning the same thing as spirit. Or ever read anything about God's blind side? I don't hardly see where the carnal every considered such a thing as a blind side of a spirit.

Let me run you by a little parable here. Let's say you were talking to someone on your left side looking left, laid your hand to your right-on top of a very hot stove to sort of lean on just a little. If you felt no pain after a few minutes God might think you were sending him a sweet-smelling sacrifice, get it? We are just not created like a spirit and do not have many of its features.

Then I read in Revelations of a point where God declared there will be no more time and no more pain. Former things are passed away, the carnal will be gone. We are the tail, as long-as we are in the carnal, but in the spirit, we can be the head with God.

God says that his people can be the head and not the tail, if we will just choose his Spirit. We will be elevated above the angels. Jesus said, "The words I speak, they are Spirit and they are life."

I could write a lot that the Bible says about hell, but that is not my purpose for this book. I'm trying to reveal God, not hell, just that if God made a heaven, he made a hell. Every one of us is destined to spend eternity in one place or the other. We have a choice but God holds the keys, we must deal with him. He is very merciful and has all the attributes of a righteous God but has no variations. Does not the Bible say there is no variableness in him? He is a Spirit.

This is hard for carnal man to understand. Fact is, he does not understand. Therefore, we must come to know God and trust him. (Spirit is the opposite of carnal). He said "Them that know God will put their trust in him." (Do you notice that he said that backwards to the way we think? Know God first then you will put your trust in him) He is the one that says it right, I assure you. Why would anyone that does not know him put their trust in him?

I would like to insert, I guess they would call it, one of my opinions in here. I had just received the first print of my first book for approval to be put into print. This is my 5th book I'm writing on now. (I know I'm writing a lot about myself, but I intend to make a point with this), I wrote a lot about opinions in all the other books. About how cheap they are and everybody has one. Everybody is entitled to one, and how one can pick up all he can carry, on any busy street corner in a short time and will probably not cost him a dime. But sometimes one can pick up valuable information, if he has just a little bit of spiritual discernment about him. If he can listen, more than to give the sacrifice of fools, as God put it. I think I made it plain that I believed opinions should cease when the truth comes into play and I believed that the Word of God is the truth, the whole truth, and nothing but the truth.

When the printers wrote a little description on the cover about me and the book and mentioned it as offering a lot of my opinions. Nothing big, but I kind of felt a little tug of a negative feeling. From the way, I see things when I feel like it is my opinion I try to say so and add to it, you can take it for whatever it is worth for it is just my opinion; and will probably tell what I base it on. But if I state something as a fact it's because I think I can back it up with the Bible with at least two or three conformations from the Bible. For that is the way it says to do with every word that comes out of the mouth of God.

This is the point I wanted to make with this, I will not argue but very little or stand very hard on my opinion but will stand on what the Bible says until someone shows me, by the Bible, that I am wrong. So, I think what I write and wrote is true and much more than just my opinion. That is my point and my opinion.

When I make statements that I think that are true about carnal things and people, I am willing to stand liable for any statement I make. Or willing to go to the Bible with anybody that has a sensible spirit about him. But in my thinking, anybody that don't believe the King James Bible is the Word of God, is not sensible. Show me another Bible with Jesus Christ's story and words and testimony in it, I might at least look-into it, but so far, I haven't even heard of one, except a copy maybe. I am very Leery of any copy calming the spirit and seal of Jesus Christ. God said in the beginning to not add to or diminish ought from his Word, and Jesus confirmed it very strongly; that he is that word. God is running the world by that Bible, and Daniel saw in it from his time down to the very end. Through all the future kingdoms; through the eyes of his people. And was told there would be another book written after his time.

John wrote the book of Revelations, the last book given to us, seen through the eyes of God's full kingdom, both Jews and Gentiles, down to and including the battle of Armageddon, and God the Father coming down with his glory to make his abode among men. Christ used the same beast to show John the kingdoms, as he did to show Daniel the kingdoms, a few thousand years earlier. Not a change in it, just three of the kingdoms come and gone just like Daniel said they would. Now tell me why I need another Bible, or another book, I've got one that works and is proven. But of course, man thinks he could make some improvements on it, but I do not know where or how, or any need for them. God does not need man's advice or help. But we are dead without his.

I decided years ago, that a preacher spending more time explaining the Bible away, than explaining the Bible was just wasting both mine and his time. And I don't need any preaching coming from his heart and spirit that does not line up with the Bible. Even though he may have a heart and spirit of gold, my soul is not for sell even for gold.

I am fully convinced that the Bible is the Word of God and is spiritually written and spiritually discerned. Jesus said so anyhow. It is sharper than any two-edged sword, and is a discerner of the thoughts and intents of the heart. It is a better weapon than any Russian made gun in their stockpile. And has already revealed the thoughts and intents of any beast (man power) formed on this earth with any significance concerning God's people.

People that believe in God don't have a big problem with him discerning hearts and minds of people. But to fully accept the fact that he put it into the Bible by his prophets the discernment of hearts and minds of people of today, a few thousand years ago, is a little more difficult to grasp. Proving that time doesn't mean a thing to God, only to us, he can see and know the future just as well as the past, no difference with him. This is a little hard for a carnal mind to digest, but he thinks he can instruct God. This is kind of humorous to God, he said he would set in heaven and laugh at such foolishness. Why should we marvel at that? I have seen people set in front of their goof tubes and roll in laughter at some of the most foolish things imaginable. Can we not allow God a little space even though he does not require it? What about all the cheering and laughter at Miley Rae Cyrus, of course that was exciting, do you think God thought so? I doubt it, but he does have some humor.

The thing carnal has such a hard time with, is simply the fact that God is everything and does not need man in any form, and man is demanding that he prove it. Well he is going to, and he is not going to lose one thing. And is not going to take our little dab of time on this earth to prove it to seven billion people every day when they get up to start their day. He has the time, but we don't. And his Word is not going to change or diminish one bit nor should we add one thing to it. Everything has been declared already and being fulfilled down to the last word, in heaven. I have no idea why man thinks he can get by or around it. Seems the only way he can come up with is to rewrite the Bible and ignore the one that has already been written, or claim that an older one is its equal or more.

I don't see any possibilities of man succeeding with either one. Especially after considering how long he has been trying to do it and has not been able to change one word of approved, or authenticated scripture. Jesus told his disciples, you did not choose me, I chose you. God told Pharaoh, "For this purpose I raised you up to show my power to the world." In other words, Pharaoh did not choose to grow into being Pharaoh, God raised him up for that purpose. He just lusted after the position. He says he ordains every power being given to man, anywhere.

What man was setting in on all that planning? Seems to me there was probably not one single one there. When will man, with his pea brain, ever wake up? He only has one of two sides to get on, a righteous God that is a Spirit, or a lying, rebellious spirit that has been defeated and is powerless to lay a hand on man. Except in his mind and man must consent to that for all it has-to offer is to please our lust when that is nothing but a lie. Or to try to scare us to accepting their god by cutting off our heads. But if you are not afraid of them that is not likely.

Our God has said if we will stand as one with him, then he will stand with us. Everything a false god can promise is headed toward death and hell.

Any or every promise a false god can make is toward the carnal lust, for that is the only things that is attractive to the carnal. But the carnal is not going to make it into the next world, so why try to lay up for it there? For it is not going to ever see the next world. Can it see a spirit here? Or even feel one? Oh, it thinks it can, but it is a sucker and easy to fool for it is a fool. Ever hear the saying; there is no fool like an old fool? Man, has had plenty of time and practice at being a fool. I believe he could be counted to be qualified for an old fool.

All the wisdom of man is put under the foolishness of God, does not even register to him. Carnal man, doesn't ever get anything right, always backwards, and wrong. His only chance is to believe God and listen to him. The truth will set you free, nothing else will.

What did the Jews say about Jesus? If we listen to him, we will lose our whole country. So, they killed him, what happened? They lost their whole country, seems they had already lost it and didn't have enough sense to see it. People think if they listen to God today they will lose everything, but just the opposite is true. Without faith and hope they have already lost everything, and just cannot see it. Can you not see why God uses the expression, wake up and open your eyes? Or open your eyes and wake up?

God has saved the Jews and set them back up, all up through the Old Testament. So many times, it got to sounding like a broken record or a needle hung in the groove. They just would not hear or obey him. When you live in the flesh and cannot see above and beyond the carnal. You are a looser and about have only the friends you can buy or that can buy you, or can control you some other way. So, he told them what he was going to do and did it. They missed Jesus, the one he sent, because of partial blindness and to give everyone an equal opportunity to receive him. Even though he warned them so plainly, they still have a chance to walk with God with every need met. If they could just say (With a whole heart), blessed is he that cometh in the name of the Lord. Jesus said if you were ever to receive him and the Father, you must receive the ones he sends, it is the same thing. The Jews that are dead and gone and the others, I cannot speak for them, except I am sure they had their opportunity.

Therefore, I stress heavy you have-to know the Spirit of God and yield to it and learn to be led by it. You cannot do it on your own or for anybody else. But if you are sincere God will send you all the help you need if you are humble and have a contrite spirit of your own. That is what he meant when he said that to the Jews, and it is the same message to everybody in the world. He has always been the same, never has changed and never will.

But until they do, their house will be left unto them desolate and every nation on earth will be led up against them. This includes America, one of the biggest ducks in the puddle. I've always knew this was going to happen because God plainly said it would. But when I was younger I could not see how it could come about in a nation that was, *fearful of God and acknowledged him in almost everything*. But now it has become to us as a bright light to them that can see; that we don't have a smidgen bit of either one left in us.

God said he would deal with every people the same way as they dealt with Israel which is God's chosen people. And the very fig tree that he told every one of us to pray for and to watch and see the nearness of his coming. They are our example. Like God said, this country gets farther away from God and Israel every day because we hate Jesus Christ, and Truth, which is the same thing. This country is following down the same path that the Jews walked down even with all the warnings God's Word has given us; and Israel, for an example. How can we be so stupid and blind? It is easy when that is what we are. The blind leading the blind and will both fall in the ditch, or pit, the same thing.

Let us go back and look a little closer at what God fully said, he would treat any one the same way as they treated Israel, his people. That must mean he will treat us the same way as his people or as he has treated Israel, even said for us to look at Israel as an example.

The reason we have been brought so low, and going so much lower is, we have accepted our government as our God, and teacher, and to raise our children. Just what he told us not to do. God said when we get into trouble, he will tell us to look to the god we serve to meet our needs. That is just what he is doing, why are we complaining? We chose it for our God, what did we expect? For it to supply or Godly needs? Ever think, maybe we need to look to a different God? Like maybe the one that created us, instead of a man-made god and government. They are a very small substitute for the real God. Worth thinking on for a while; but will not help you any if not acted upon. The only way to receive it is to put our trust in him. Someday man will learn that God is running everything. But for the most it is going to be too late.

CHAPTER 6

EVERYONE IS ENTITLED TO THEIR OPINION

Muslim or Islam religion, have no intent or desire to be equal or contemporary with any other religion in the world. But to totally dominate the entire world and kill, steal, or destroy anyone of any other religion. Most of all, the Christian and Jews religion. They are the perfect Antichrist and could never fit under our constitution or in our country without annihilation of the people that occupy it now. And that is against our constitution. They well know it, and fully intend to do just that to take over this country, and the world. They can only make laws to their own religion and cannot apply them to any other religion; goodness knows how hard they try. This is what freedom of religion means. No religion has a right to pass laws upon another religion. Try to hold that up under our Democrat government we have now. I had about as soon to have a Muslim over our country. *** ! + Isn't that what we have got? A Muslim and a Democrat; if I am wrong, cut my legs off and call me shorty.

Seems that this country does not know they not only have that right, but have that protection. If we will protect our constitution against our Democrat federal judges clear up to the Supreme Court; which I believe should be impeached. But do not expect our Mystery Babylon Democrat government schools to allow that to be taught to our children, they will not do it. They want to have my head cut off for teaching it to my children and I do not know any Christians that would stand up for me if they tried to do it. Of course, they would have to trump up some different charges but this administration has been known for doing just that. I guess I just have the wrong religion.

We have let the Antichrist and False Prophets preach our Bible to us until we believe that is what our Bible and constitution says. Therefore, I say I have heard enough preaching from people that cannot hear, speak or understand the Spirit of God; to do me for this lifetime.

The Antichrist and False Prophet have already taken over our colleges, courts, law making branches in congress, and everything else you can see. Flying their God hating black Muslim flag, but thank God, they have not done away with our Bible and constitution completely, YET!!

God is raising up the (Ten end time kingdoms; I call them) of the Middle East to save what little bit he can of this country from the Mystery Babylon Whore. We are so divided and confused we could never save our self, because we do not know what Bible to believe. Thank God, he is not going to let the False Prophet of the Mystery Babylon Whore, mother of all harlots and abominations of the earth, unite with the Antichrist of the East. Only for a short while, not long enough to take Israel off the map. That will give us a little time to pull ourselves together and repent. They will be the major ones fighting these wars and rumors of wars Jesus was talking about in these end times. For them that can be woke up and see the light before it is too late. We would be smart to stay out of as many of them as possible, but protecting our own country and Israel.

Jesus is gone to prepare us a place and promised to come back to us that have made themselves ready. We have not made us a safe place here on this earth that he gave to us. How could we, when each one of us is fighting the other one? He sent back his spirit living in us now and with us every minute, yet we don't know him and still can't believe him. You can see we are facing the exact same things today he described to us and told us about two thousand years ago, that's enough to convince me that he is not a changing God, unfaithful, seeing things different every day. That is us, not God.

God gives us a Godly man to guide us and lifts us back on our feet a little, but two terms is all he can stand up to the selfish God hating establishment trying to impeach and kill him and beating him down. Blaming the things, they were doing on him until they get the lovers-of-self world to hating him. So, he gives us another God Hating Democrat to rub our face in our own filth, until now we owe the rest of the world our very souls; which has got us worshiping their god. And telling us daily that they are going to kill us even if they must come and get us, if we don't surrender to them now.

Any government that has, and acknowledges God as the head, will work together and be blessed and prosper. While any government that does not will fail, and will have oppression and give oppression, God says so, and proving it all over the world every day. Where, is a safe place to live among that kind of people? They are Devil possessed.

A president hopeful, George McGovern, a little before his time, wanted to do away with our military, told us so before Bill and Hillary came along. When somebody ask him, what if they invaded us here in our own country? His reply was, "If we meet them on our shores with flowers instead of guns then no one would get hurt." This has been the Democrats plan to win wars and elections ever since. It has won elections but I cannot, and have not, seen it winning a war. I guess we should have met them 9-11 pilots on our shores with flowers. Look at the lives we would have saved. In fact, that is what we done. Glenn Beck has adopted that message lately; I do not know who converted him. It must have been Satan, or one of his democrat imps. I just about cannot watch him anymore.

President Johnson said we would (Spend our way into prosperity.) I think he was thinking we could spend our way out of wars too, from the way they run the Vietnam and Korea Wars. Democrats warned us to not act tuff to them devil worshipers. That has been the Democrat's philosophy ever since. Now they are telling us it's our fault, they told us so, and we should have listened to them and surrendered a long time ago. I cannot convince myself just what their problem is, I cannot believe they are that stupid even though they can sell it to most voters after sending them to their brain washing schools. I have trouble believing they hate God that much, to just throw a nation of God loving people down in the mud just to have someone to blame. The only thing I can kindly settle on is they just lust after the lies, power, fame, and easy money so much they will sell this nation down into hell for the short time of glory and money they receive. Obama, has used more than, ten trillion dollars, selling our country to the world.

I have trouble speaking foreign languages. I have served and visited in several foreign countries, it's difficult to understand them. The Democrats have refused to allow English to be declared our official language and trying to make us learn to speak Spanish in our schools right now. I reckon it's because the Bible, the Constitution, the Declaration of Independence are written in English; and they hate it, and them.

The Whore Church, the beast rider of the 17th chapter of Revelations, will have scored a biggest victory yet in its battle if it can make the English Language a dead language. No wonder the Muslims and illegal aliens' love our politicians so much. It is also no wonder why the Democrats love them and all the other God haters so much. They keep them assured of a glorious job and paycheck, and money coming from China and many terrorist countries. In the form of a loan.

Now the Democrats are riding high on plenty of money and vacations for the ones that are running things in Washington but wait until Allah gets their flag over our capital and don't need them greedy, lying blood sucking cowards any more. They will be the first ones killed, especially the hypocritical ones that are claiming to be Christians. The False Prophet leading the Mystery Babylon Whore Church has subtly moved into charged of our country and eased our Bible (Jesus Christ) out and teaming up with the Antichrist thinking they are going to rule the world again. But Jesus has other plans.

The only thing I cannot understand is where are the real Christians at? I refuse to believe they are just that stupid, so about the only thing I can come up with is they just are not out there. When God spoke of a falling away just before

Jesus comes back, I began to think that might have been a big understatement on God's part. It is looking more like a train wreck, than just a falling away. He did call it a *great* falling away; and said the world would follow-after that Antichrist; so, I guess he covered it. I will write some more on this in another place.

My philosophy is that any person that is not willing to stand up and fight for this great country of freedom and opportunity ought not to be allowed to live here in it. That includes a president and congressman and a turn coat secretary of state, that wants to throw into prison the people that are willing to stand up and lay their life on the line for our country and its God given liberties that are outlined in our constitution; that they want so bad to do away with. They turn lose all their leaders that we capture and give them hundreds of billions of dollars and arms to help them kill more women, Christians, Jews and children. I'll accept and support that over my dead body.

Does today's Christians believe our Bible is written by the Muslim's god and says that God's people that carry the name of his Son should just work their backsides off and give it to foreigners, law breakers, gangsters, dope addicts, liars, blasphemers, murderers, rapist, worshipers of some of the worst murdering false gods the world has ever seen. *I am talking about our liberal Democrats.* Telling us we can earn our way to heaven by doing these things. Somebody has lost their marbles, if they ever had any.

If that is the way Obama learned our Bible while he was going all the years to Rev. Wright's church surely somebody had spilled ink on their Bible. Surely, something must have happened to it. I would have tried to help them to raise enough money to have bought a readable Bible if they would have just said something about it. I've never heard them come up with even that flimsy of an excuse for blaspheming and lying about my Bible. I'm not sure they ever read from the King James Bible. I'm sure I've never heard either of them preaching from it, except to say that *our* God says to kill our children and *our* God says, God dam America. But I know very few Christians that do any better, and preaching we have the same God as the Muslims do.

If anybody wants to rise and come at me for speaking truth, just choose your weapon. You might remember they killed Jesus, his disciples, and the prophets for the same things, and we count them to have made it. I wonder what the ones made that killed them. A place in history for sure. As Saul Lewinsky and Hillary says, they successfully built their own kingdom as Lucifer did. I just added a little food for thought for the ones that can still think. It is starting to seem that number is getting very small and scarce.

But I believe I have figured out the reason why it is so hard to tell anyone anything anymore. Everybody is so busy interrupting and trying to tell everybody else what they know, they have no time or room to hear anybody else. They certainly do not believe they have any need to hear anything from somebody else, when they are so sure that they know more than all the others, about anything. Just take the time to look and listen a while when you see another round table discussion. I believe you may be surprised at what you can learn about people.

One of them is it don't take very long to learn most of them knows very little about anything. Usually, the one that is doing the most talking, knows the least. When they started teaching our children there was no such thing as absolutes, I was one of the children in the schools at the time. I told them then, in the early fifties, it was just an underhanded, sleazy, way of saying there was no such thing as a God. I did not buy it then and I do not buy it now.

If you are wondering how I justify myself after making such bold talk? I am not claiming any wisdom of my own, just what I can back up by the Word of God and can see, try proving him wrong, join the world, break a leg as they say. Thousands of years and they don't have much fruit to show for their labor, and things just go right on happening like he said it would in the beginning. Even after whipping them in two world wars, we have let them win just like they said they would. If you can have me killed it will not change a thing. Look at the ones they have killed from the beginning of time and the Word of God is still just as strong as ever. But we have lost our Bibles. Mystery Babylon from the beast in Rome have threw them out the windows when they took over our schools, and now our government.

You may not be able to read this book, the printers that has done some of my books are telling me they are not going to print this one if I do not remove some of the criticism of the president and several others from it. I don't know if they will be able to shut down my freedom of speech or not, they sure have been trying for several years. I think I still have it. I guess we will see, for I intend to get it done if I possibly can, and I do not intend to strip it out for them.

I learned from a wise fellow long ago how to break into a discussion. You get their attention and say, now fellows, if you want to hear this story you are going to have to shut up and listen. Well, that might be getting a little rude like them. But it is for sure that to fully be accepted as interesting to talk to by someone else, you must talk about things he is interested in. Almost no one is interested in a spiritual creator that is not interested in his lust, pleasure, greedy, selfish, accomplishments, and his great success stories, and lies that set him above God. That just about leaves a man of God out of any of the conversations even in most churches and church gatherings, so the only time a preacher is needed is at weddings or for a funeral, and then only if they send for him.

They will scrip to him what they want him to say, he had better be careful how he says anything for the spirit of anything determines the meaning, or power, that goes with each word. They want no word said, coming from the wrong spirit. That usually means from truth or from Jesus Christ the same thing. This holds true in anything when you are dealing with people. Why do you think so few people go to church anymore? Unless that preacher is tuning his sermons to the same spirit that they are of, which is almost never from the Holy Ghost; they are not interested. Only when they are both in the Spirit of God can or will they ever come together as one, in agreement or anything else, in the same building.

God's Spirit calls us together as one, in one mind, one accord, one judgment, one voice even one body, members one of another. Of course, that is talking in and of and from the Spirit as all the Bible is; all the time. If you are a child of God, you need to get used to it. A carnal spirit is left out of the Spirit of God, so that means the Spirit of God is left out of the carnal. I don't know who to blame, as there is nothing to gain in finding blame, but I know who the looser is.

The other spirit that is contrary (or backwards) to God is calling us to the opposite side of God, which is to divide and conquer, to take total control. Jesus said if you are not gathering with us you are scattering abroad. If you are not working with the Spirit of God, you are scattering, not gathering anything. Which spirit do you think politicians are of? I would not think one should have any doubt.

I know that the false gods are saying that of the real God and trying to make him out to be the false god and to blame for everything bad and wrong, why not? The Democrats have had that working for them since they lost the Civil War, improving upon it every election. Even to the convincing of the country that the Republicans started the war and was the father of the KKK, and was hanging black Democrats. Truth is over half the men the KKK hung were white, and every one of them were Republicans. The names were taken off a KKK list of names for hanging that was recovered later. Anyone that would believe that God's name is Allah, should be easy to convince of the other things. It would seem they have no problem in that area. But I don't believe they can convince God or his people that he is one and the same with Allah. If they can convince his people that, I don't believe they will be his people any longer. If you do not want to believe truth, and love and help a lie instead, God says you will be dammed. That would make Rev. Wright a correct preacher, when he said, "Its God Da-America." I don't feel qualified to argue with him. But I don't believe we will be dammed for killing ungodly people, more apt for not killing enough of them.

God gave his people the command to kill certain ones. But later gave them rebuke for killing the ones he wanted to keep alive, and keeping alive the ones he wanted killed. The obvious problem is not knowing when a person is godly or ungodly and not knowing and obeying the Word and Spirit of God. How could we if we don't know God, who is a Spirit? As I've wrote and preached several times, God is not a variable God.

God communicates to us through revelations, not much, by the same way as we talk to one another. Not that he can't, it's just so tremendously far below the Spirit of God, and when he tried to speak to man in man's carnal language men were getting it all twisted up and confused. Therefore, he gave us the King James Authorized Translation that he said he himself wrote and he wanted not a word added to it or one in it to be changed at all. And when we try to instruct him he finds it humorously insulting to himself. It makes us look and sound very foolish. God is full of pity and patience, but if anything could wear him out I'm sure earthy, fleshly humans could. He says the flesh is warring with the spirit, and knowledge is worrisome to the flesh. Many things don't fit well together without some friction, especially when they are moving in different directions.

He has given us a Bible full of wisdom and revelations. Plain as day if we could just attain an open mind and common sense. But we are just about void of both and not getting any better with time. Every revelation is there for a purpose and for our learning. Every parable, every story, every fact stated is there for our education and our school housing. And is the truth the whole truth and nothing but the truth. Now tell me that man wrote it? I might just laugh in your face.

So, the Babylon Whore books that we give to our children, teach that it is so foolish and dangerous to our kids that the Bible is outlawed. Look where our kids are at. Do you reckon the false church of Revelations, seventeenth chapter, the one God called the Mother of Abominations and Harlots of the earth; rider of the beasts of the earth might have something to do with it? Having ruled over kings and nations; drunk on the blood of the saints and martyrs of Jesus from having killed well over a hundred million of Jesus's saints, for being caught with a piece of scripture. Or attempting to teach anything about the Word of God not being approved by them; might be somewhat to blame? Do you think it could have influenced the way we think about Jesus Christ and the Word of God in this country today? They are running our schools, printing our curriculum, changing our history. They have tried to stomp out the Bible throughout all their entire history of existence. We defeated them soundly in two world wars, but did not annihilate them like God has told his people to do. Now we are serving them, in every way.

We are acting the very same way and teaching so. God said when he destroyed the final Babylon; he found the blood of all the saints; and all the blood that had been shed on the earth, in her. Read about it in the 18th chapter of the book of Revelations, and the results in the 19th and 20th chapters. A question I would love to hear some smart preacher to ponder over a little, if he didn't fear for his life too much, to speak truth.

All that I have said here in the past few pages, I have not judged one person, but God has judged every single person by this Word of God I quoted. We are told every one of us, to judge ourselves by it. It has already judged us, we just need to read it and know the way it judged us, while we still have some time to prepare ourselves. Killing the preacher will not help or change a thing.

Any teaching that does not align with the Word of God is just wrong, is just about all that can be said about it. Our so-called scientist, (Paul says, falsely so accused) just needs to wake up. I know of no place they have proved God to be wrong, not even when they taught the world was flat and the sun went around the earth and huge animals made the oil and gases of the earth. The Bible teaches the animals and everything else on and around the earth is made up out of elements from the earth, not the other way around. I am not convinced that one man or animal was present when God created the earth and hung the sun out on nothing and placed the stars with his fingers and named every one of them.

Job didn't know where he was at when it all took place, God ask him. And we are to believe that God did all that and had no man there, even to advise him? sic. Very unbelievable don't you think? I'm sure O'Reilly and Goldburg cannot believe that for I've heard them say they don't. And they are not a rare couple, by any means, they have many agreeing with them but God says not to go with the multitude. That is a very poor excuse to call God a lair, just because the multitude loves to hear it.

So, mankind can be divided into two sides, the carnal and the spiritual. Each side is divided into many factions, every faction on the carnal side is lost, and on their way to hell. Not judging, just stating what the Bible teaches. "I judge no man," that is the words of Jesus; I believe I can repeat them. But he tells each of us to judge ourselves, and we are to do that by the Bible for it has already judged everything. So, when we read it correctly or hear it taught correctly all we must do is look at ourselves, we should know ourselves better than anybody else. If we will be honest with our self and believe the Word of God, we should be able to know just exactly where we are at.

God's word calls that a righteous judgment. The problem with most people is, it is harder to be honest with self than to somebody else, especially when it is about self. Most people have a hard time just being honest period. God calls them lairs and has condemned them that cannot receive truth, all to have their part in the lake of fire. I am glad God told me I did not have to judge whether everything I hear is true or not. I believe that would be an unfair assignment.

But I am responsible for what I believe and support and love. He has told me things to not believe and ways to check many things out. I believe patients and common sense with a little wisdom may be one of the best combinations of advice. Man, has come a long way by his own measurements, but we haven't moved in with God yet. Or even found where he lives at in heaven; even though they have been trying hard too. I would say I don't believe they ever will but they would say that many said that man would never fly.

But God has said much about man soaring on wings like an eagle long before they invented a machine that could fly. I don't believe they slipped anything upon God, like a surprise or something. He can look at the future just as plain as he can see the past. And he has not said much about man showing up in his home for a surprise visit with no invitation and taking his seat away from him.

He has spoken of several heavens and I'm sure he could find one to hide in, if he found it necessary to escape from man. I cannot phantom him being very worried about that situation. And I've never read where he said anything like he had a worry that something might jump up that he could not handle.

God is too big for the heavens and earth to contain him, taller than the stars, no power given that he did not ordain. Makes me wonder what they are going to tie him up with when they get him captured. I am sure a bunch of cartoon writers could come up with something that could hold him.

They came up with kryptonite for Superman, I known, for Obama said he was born in it, but not in a manger. That apparently sounded smart to a lot of people, but I thought it sounded like a sick calf to me.

To understand anything about God or his creation, the Bible is where it is all at. Scientist has been known to change their minds every few years, several times even in my lifetime alone. But I have never known of God changing, and he says he never will, he will always remain the same. Even if he decided to change, we would never know about it for he would never change toward us. Not that he would cheat, he doesn't have to, he doesn't need to. He is everything and if he changed everything would be changed, so, how would we know anything about it, if he did not tell us.

Anytime you talk about God you must talk in a circle. You can rant all you want to, where are you going? You can only come right back to where you started from, for there is where you are at. Any time you get away from God, you are lost until you get back. The only way to get back is where you got off or away from God at. He will always be right there where you left him, he is not going anywhere. This is what he means when he says he never changes. When you get back you will find the same God you tried to rant and run away from. For you never went anywhere anyway.

You may have changed, and hopefully you have and to the better, but you will not have changed one thing about God, not even taught him one thing about yourself. He knew everything before you left and he still knows everything, so what are you going to add to him? We are just like puppets in God's hands so why not try to please him. He may just drop the strings if we don't.

Look how long the Jews have been fighting God, and have not learned this truth that I just explained, they are our example. He has told them and us all these things. How long is it going to take for either one of us to learn about God? The sad truth is the clear majority of the both of us never will, and Jesus will not know nor claim us when we all stand before him and his Father. It will be a sad day for billions of people, and many of them have already pictured themselves leaving this earth gloriously with their feet still on them and never to stand before judgment. I heard Billy Graham preach once, that he was living his eternal life now and would never have to stand before God in judgement. Sounded good, but I wondered what he done with the scripture where God said, it was appointed unto man once to die and then the judgment.

I'm still looking in my Bible for that story and if I find it I'll still have to find the two or three witnesses in God's Word to establish it. So far, I have not found anything about it except F. Jennings Dake, and Jimmy Swagger's writings which are plainly adding to the Word of God, which God said not to do. When I hear, a preacher preaching what and how God "HAS" to do something, using carnal reasoning to place him in that corner, he has lost me. My Bible says God sets in heaven and does as he pleases. I take that to mean no preacher is going to be able to tell God what he, *has,* to do.

They can preach all day that God will do what he says he is going to do. I've never read where he said he would have to kill a certain group of people just for getting caught in a certain time-period. I have read where he has his way in a whirl wind. Name me some place where he cannot have his way. I read where a thousand could be slain on my left hand and ten thousand on my right and not come near my dwelling place. Where do they find that God, *has,* to slay me if I don't make the rapture?

I talked with a small business man the other day (I build most of my writings and sermons on listening to people). He said that President W. Bush was a complete idiot. I ask him to explain a little, or coming from where, did he see that? He said, "Coming from anywhere that was all he could see in him was just a lot of [hot air] was all he was." I ask him if the kicking of Afghanistan and Iraq up straight a little, and the hanging of Saddam, and the killing of hundreds that was ranking high in the group that committed 9-11 was just a lot of hot air? He said, well, that was just his opinion and he was entitled to his opinion. I agreed but told him I agreed with Glenn Beck that opinions should cease when truth was presented.

Well, we talked some more but in thinking; I got hung up a little on the words "hot air." I believe the hot air was coming from the other side and he was burned up with too much of it. The main source of it from CBS, NBC, ABC, CNN, and all their affiliates promoting their Hate Bush campaign. Vigorously fed by left headed Idealist liars; like Al Gore, Senator Kennedy, Clintons, Pelosi, Reid and all the other selfish God haters that supported and voted for them. Like college teachers that God has turned over to a reprobate mind with strong delusions to believe any good sounding lie and be dammed. Because they do not love truth, and certainly don't know how to teach it. Read about it in the first chapter of the book of Romans, and backed up several other places, in the Bible.

How about Al's book he made a few million on and shook up the left headed world with. Had the north pole cap melting and flooding the rest of the world with about half the U S under water, due to have been done around ten years ago, had the head hunting, God hating news stations beating their drums and doing their spirit dances. Speaking of Hot Air, I could quote many more examples but I think, that one should about take the cake, and coming from the left, they get dull and boring quickly; not to mention a little sickening.

They think they have found something new about earth warming? Why don't they read their Bible? God said the earth would wax old and ware out like a dirty shirt. It says God is going to scorch men with the sun, and later burn up the whole creation. I don't believe Obama or Gore is going to do one thing about that.

I've told everybody for years, I knew what the BS stood for in the CBS, but was a little confused about the C. I had heard the story told on president, Giv'em Hell Harry Truman, shortly after he took office. He was very liberal at calling anything unappealing to him a very plain "BS." Some of his associates spoke to his wife and ask her to speak to Harry and explain to him that it was not very appropriate for a president to be calling things that. She said, you better just leave Harry alone, you should have heard what he called it before he became president.

I knew what BS meant but had been pondering on the C for some time. I had thought of the word, uncontrolled, but that didn't start with a C and didn't fit in very well, but after him telling me about that, *hot air,* I realized that the C is not uncontrolled, but well Controlled. The hot air is very close to Harry's BS, don't know why it took me so long to see it. Just not very quick witted I guess. Now I know what the C.B.S. stands for and the other newsmen are not very far behind, if any.

They were good at it, got the world blaming Reagan for all the problems, saying he started them by starting up the longest continuous economic growth in our history. Bush, because he paid out the card holders and the banks for the money that was spent during Clinton's time. So, everybody had some of the best times under Clinton they ever had, calling him the best president we ever had. Ask any Democrat. No wonder God said people was so foolish; he knew it to be so, didn't have to figure it out. Clintons and Obamas may be good enough liars to fool the world but I don't believe they fooled God for one minute. I really don't believe they fooled God's people, they didn't fool me and I barely have enough intelligence to get by.

I told them loud and clear when Clinton was first elected that this country or the Democrat party one, was going down. And if they stuck together it might take longer but they would both be going down. I meant all the way down, not just a bobber bouncing up and down a little. We, with any godly principles, struggled through two terms of Bill and Hillary, God gave them to us, for it was the people that wanted them. Some on the left after the election, knowing how I voted, loved to sort of gloat it over me just a little, I had several comebacks for them. One yelled, "What do you think of our president" I said, "I think he is just as much my president as he is yours and I can certainly stand him if you can, I can spend that government money just as easy as the next man" But think God I didn't spend my head under water like so many others did, even though I received a few checks from a few of them banks in the amount of four to five thousand dollars telling me all I had to do was just take them to a bank and sign them on the back and pick up my money. I threw them into the burn trash. The Democrats had the printing presses oiled up and rolling out that money at record speed.

After a few years of that, I could easily see why there were record numbers of bankruptcies being filed. It had nothing to do with me being much smarter than so many of the others as to see ahead what was coming; it was just that I was not as blatantly greedy and stupid as so many of them.

Why worry when you can blame it on the stupid Republicans and get them run out of Washington, and more Democrats elected? At least Bill didn't do it from Hawaii and Martha's Vineyard, and on the golf course. I guess he did his vacations in the white house, playing with his cigar.

We had Newt Gingrich to keep him from running us into oblivion but we don't have him to protect us now. The Democrats, and the main stream news reporters run him out of Washington. Leaving us defenseless with a few Republicans scared to open their mouth or they would be run off by the news media, colleges or federal judges, or if needed, by the FBI and IRS or NSA. Our country was run down worse than it was under Carter, maybe as low as it had ever been. Certainly, with more debt than it had ever had. Even with Newt Gingrich balancing the budget, one year; by riding Bill like a bull.

Then God gave us W. Bush, against the will of the people. I said, God would not drop this country under a Godly man as Bush. I said, if we get so bad God thinks he needs to let us go, he will call George Bush home first. Bush fought at least three wars in his first six years in office, Afghanistan, Iraq and the Democrat party with federal money, trying to make him fail at everything he tried to do. Especially the wars and were willing to throw down the whole country just to get back in control of Washington, and finely did. When they could not make the wars to fail, and could not get impeachment charges against Bush to stick, they went to plan B.

Dropped the whole countries financial system. With the help of the colleges, complete news media scaring the old people and blacks to death, illegal voting, and airways jammed with lies, and ever vote that could be bought or stolen, they blamed it all on Bush and Reagan. Finely set Washington on fire like a barn full of hay. God pulled Bush out before it burned down. They succeeded in blaming Bush anyway, but look at the shape it has the country in now. They are still blaming it all on Reagan and Bush and Christian conservatives for it. They did it all after getting the whole of Washington DC back, at the start of Bush's last two years and they are clean as a hound's tooth. Just half of the country had to believe them; can you not see all that, clear? If you don't you are just not looking, just hearing Democrat lying liberals. That will leave you with an empty head, every time.

After the election, Pelosi, still campaigning and gloating big, going into the congress to pick up the gavel, announced that for the next election they had a plan and was going to take back the Whitehouse. The plan was to break the financial back of the whole country and blame it on the conservatives, Christians, and the white male Republicans with their guns. And she did, to the tune of over twenty trillion dollars, and more in obligations, owning to whose figures you are looking at, but they took back the Whitehouse, putting Obama in it. With a few million-dollars to her husband in California to save a little fish that nobody had ever heard of, I am still not sure it ever existed, and a military escorted trip to Europe and California threw in I reckon. They put new bearings in the printing press there in Washington, maybe even a new model. You might could see it if they ever slow it down enough to see.

Hollywood, New York, Chicago told us all real clear, what a great convenience it was to everybody, enough to put Obama in two turns and filled Washington up with help to do the job she would do. That should have convinced anybody, and did the Democrats including the Supreme Court. Obama is looking for a third term, and with our money and Democrat lies, I would not be surprised if he doesn't buy it. His last term election just cost us a few billion dollars. The liberals thought that was a bargain. I wonder.

If they cannot swing that, Hillary is waiting smugly in the wing with a five-billion-dollar purse for her turn. Obama spending ten billion dollars that we did not have. How can they lose?

The story is almost the same thing with Clinton and Bush and Reagan just a little less plain than the one we are looking at now. We can see them through hind sight. God's people didn't wake up under Reagan or little Bush. So, God has given us the most ungodly, God hating, American hating, self-declared Antichrist Muslim that didn't even constitutionally qualify to be on the ballet. Telling us plainly he was going to tear us down to a third-rate country or lower, denied we had any exceptions. Saying he would disarm us, scatter what wealth we had across the world. Disowned our flag, refused to honor it in any way, announced, against two Supreme Court decisions, that this was not a Christian nation anymore. Proved it by outlawing the Bible. While his brethren are telling us all over the world that they are going to tear down our flag and fly their flag over our capital.

Our Supreme Court is encouraging them by blessing them for burning our flag, renaming it a "Grand Free Speech." With plenty of free prime TV time with protection, while they are making it unlawful to mention Christ or the Bible on are near government property. And seems nobody can understand why I dislike Democrats? I do not believe that I am the one that is stupid or crazy. I believe they got their interpretation on free speech a little bit confused. I also believe our Supreme Court should be impeached; and our government is Devil possessed. Maybe they will get their chance to lock me in jail if they can get Hillary in.

If we keep worshiping Obama's god, the only glimmer of hope we have on the horizon is communist countries, mainly China and the atheist countries like Russia, and they are going to be at war with each other before it is over. It doesn't matter which side we get on they both hate us. We have given up our weapons and technology, like the missile guiding system that China Gate sold to China for the money to buy a New York senator's seat in congress for one of their biggest hopefuls, Hillary.

We have given Islam all our weapons, and money to help them kill Jews and Christians. Who needs us? I do not believe we can say God does. He has us and I don't believe he knows just what to do with us. But I read my Bible and he has told us very plainly just what he is going to do with us, and it doesn't look very promising. God's wrath is just a little above our heads and he is defiantly going to start pouring it out. We have grown sick of fighting for our God given liberties, forgetting we have them in the center of a God hating human race of foolish people that think the liberty of God is not worth fighting for while the freedom *from* God is worth fighting for to the death. I don't know how you could get things any more backwards or farther from truth and Christian philosophy, or God's help than that. And heaps of them claiming to be Christians. If it wasn't so sad and pitiful and dangerous, that could be good for a laugh.

Right now, we are watching the ten kingdoms rise that is going to rule the world, for a short time, which has Obama's religion and god, swiftly becoming ours. We are even outlawing Christ from our entire country and changing his name to Allah and teaching the Koran in our schools where the Bible is not allowed. This comes mostly from the Beast Riding Church in Revelations, God says so. The title of Christian is being substituted "For, Kill." I reckon God's, so called people are just as happy as a bunch of roosters fighting each other to the death. I sure do not see one that wants to fight the ones that have declared to kill us, and doing it every day.

Christians are ready to fight one another to the death at a whim but when the real enemy comes along they just all at once do not believe in fighting. Crying, "Who can fight against this man," just like God said they would. They are talking about The Antichrist, they been looking for him as a man, all my lifetime. Well, he is not a man but a spirit, about taken over every man, and been in their face since John wrote the book of revelations. They are just blind and cannot see him.

Do you reckon its cowardice or just plain lack of faith, or maybe they just feel like their soul is not worth a fight with an enemy that is willing to fight back? Or maybe it is a reprobate mind like God said it was. God said that those with no god at all would fight harder for their god than his people that have a real God would fight for Him. If your god is not worth standing up for, and fighting for if necessary,

I'd like to recommend to you the one I serve, I think him to be well worth fighting for, even to the death. I do not say that everybody should carry a gun but they sure should support the ones that are willing to. This is a real war, and there are people being killed. Whose side are you on?

Muslims are killing themselves and other people every day for their god. I think just as much of my God as they do of theirs. And they are not the same God. I remember when most of this country felt the same way, but they are hard to find anywhere now. I guess we have fought for the wrong God these few centuries; we have convinced our children we had the wrong God. And are spitting in the face of our veterans, that fought and died to build this country with every freedom you are enjoying. I find that is going to be our ruination, and I find it to also be disgusting. Where are the Christians at? If they would read their Bible, they could find out where they are at. This is what this book is about. But somebody that won't read their Bible will not want to read this book. They will about all tell you they read their Bible every day, I believe them kind will lie about other things too.

But I have decided if you are a good enough liar you can become President. Bill and Hussein did; Hillary thinks she is going too.

If lying and government money can do it, I suppose she is going to make it. Listen to them that are on the gravy train. If Trump don't make it, you can know it was the government gravy train that stopped him. I will give my signature to that message. That gravy train is going to cause God to have to enlarge hell to accept all the people that are rushing into it. I wonder what their hurry is? They are very well attached to the gravy train. I guess the top spots in hell are for people that can hurry, and hell will not be any cooler for them that are in a lesser position. I do not believe, anyway.

I can give anybody a sound reason to vote for Trump. If for no other reason, he does not need our government's money. The old establishment knows that, and he will not be catering much to their big habit of carrying all the gravy that they are so used to, so easily and for so long. That is the reason for the career politicians. They have a big addiction habit. And you should know the ones that do? None of them are about to limit their terms for themselves. Who doesn't love a gravy train once he is on it? Just don't try to tell me their interest is in my country, I do not want to hear it. I might just think you are a liar and a fool, with your eyes and ears stopped up.

CHAPTER 7

GOVERNMENT FOR GOD, HOW'S THAT WORKING OUT?

We elected them that we have, to be our commanders and chiefs and send them to Martha's Vineyard, Hawaii and Europe to vacation until their heart is content while they are freeing and arming terrorist to kill Christians. I do not understand why, just know it is so.

Does just hating truth that much justify us to love lies that much? And teach them to our children as truths. Seems to me that somebody that had no god at all, but just loves himself more than anybody else in the world, would have more respect for just a fact than most Christians I know. They don't have to call it truth, just call it a fact and go on.

Democrats are the best in the world at renaming dead things and putting life back in them with a different face. I remember when gays used to be called queers and were considered sick. The famous ACLU started out being a communist organization until it was drove underground by the Republicans, come back with a different name and face but was the same thing, much bigger in the Democrat party, trying to blame and bury Nixon and McCarthy until today, sort of like the KKK affair. There were many of them under the liberal unions that was just shifted around and renamed and kept receiving their government money, trained by Obama, the famous community organizer, and the best Democrat that could be found in the world. Even better than Hillary.

They were of course acting with a tax-free permit. Cause they were politicking for the left party. Used ten trillion dollars of tax money that we did not have, putting us that much more in debt, under Obama, along with spending all the tax money they collected to run the government on, during his entire turn. The FBI and state department had no problem with their tax permit. Any time you see a Democrat on TV, I will about steak my life on it, he will be politicking, accusing and lying, just as hard as he can. The Republicans very conveniently do not notice even when they are accusing them of every dirty thing the Democrats are guilty of. Either are afraid of getting kicked out of DC, like all the ones that had anything to do with the impeachment of Bill Clinton did, or else was too deeply involved themselves to speak out for truth. I do not know a Congressman left in Congress that had anything much to do with Bill's impeachment. They have all been sent home. By our self-loving power craving, Democrats.

I have had some, getting mad, correcting me saying, "Bill was not impeached, they only tried and could not get it done." Trying to put a new face and definition on the word impeach, and did, just ask a Democrat. He will explain it to you, I just about promise you he will probably be ready to fight over his explanation, being Christian or not. Better take along a club.

Christian voters in our country are like a Christian nation in the world situation, they do not have a side to get on and it is completely dangerous to even be called a Christian, for not even another Christian will support you. That is what makes it so dangerous. For he is sure that you are not nowhere near as good a Christian as he is, so he had rather vote for a Muslim that he knows is lying. Than take a chance on a Christian that might lie to him, and he hates because he is of another denomination. And so-called Christians are preaching to us that we must love gays and people that is sworn to kill us for their false god's namesake, or we will be called a hypocrite, instead of a Christian, and threw out of the church. We will be put in jail if he howls the *offended* word or *racists.*

They need to read what Christ called them, when they cannot even love their own brothers. Of course, they killed Christ and all his close followers. Now, we don't want that, so we are very careful. God says plainly, that they are going to hell. God says in at least two different places, "He hates all workers of inequity and vanity." "And in some things, we offend all, but woe unto them through which the offence comes." I do not need a hypocrite to tell me what my Bible says. I can give you a long list of things God says for me to hate and not to eat with, some he said to kill. All you must do is read your Bible you can see for yourself.

God said, to set a ruler over you that rules in the fear of God. I've not found much about another quality we are told to look for. I am sure he was not referring to a false god or someone who thinks he is setting in God's seat, nothing sets there but the Word of God. Anybody that blasphemes it, need not look very hard for my support or God's support either, he said so.

God will put him in office if that is what the people want and deserve. Then he will be judged when God is through with him just like the people he ruled, even with much more stern judgment because of what he was given to be responsible for. Them that are given much, much is required.

I have developed a way of voting, because I like to give my vote, which I think I am obligated to do, so I use it as an, against vote. If I cannot see fit to vote for either one, that is usually because the one I wanted did not get into the race. I can always see that one is much farther from God than the other one, usually by exercising no fear of God in anything he ever did. And giving God no credit in anything he ever accomplished. And almost always speaking blasphemy against the Bible. That man does not fear God and you can bet on it. And he has more pride than Lucifer got threw out of heaven for.

I will cast my vote against that man, even if he is as smart as Obama and promises me the moon. I am a very simple man, as Bill O' says, but I am not so stupid as to believe he is going to be able to bring the moon down here. If he could, I do not believe that he would give it to me without a lawsuit. Do you believe that I even might win a lawsuit against his attorney general with her Black Panthers to enforce the orders and court proceedings, and to control the voting booth? I am white.

How smart he is, depends on a matter of opinion. You know he would not allow his school records to be revealed. Did not have a birth certificate, got a social security number, from a dead man in a state he has never shown to have lived in and cannot explain. Of course, a Democrat is not required too. Why that was not a red flag was because them Democrat, God hating, news reporters dressed it up and run it down our stupid gullible throats, and told us it tastes good, and was just what we needed, to help our stupid Republican minds, I guess. I agree it should have, but it didn't. Seems it has got a bad after taste, but no one dares to acknowledge that for it was given to us by our glorious Democrats. Self-proclaimed expert doctors, always knows just what is good for us stupid Republicans. Guaranteed by our college teachers and lawyers and all them that they had college professors giving high marks to tell us, there cannot be one bad taste about it, it's all in your mind. There is your answer, them that had a mind of Christ with some knowledge of God would have known better from the start. Instead had their minds being turned over to a reprobate, to believe a lie and be dammed. Because they do not love truth, just like God warned and explained to us. In the first chapter of the book of Romans.

We are now in worse shape than Israel. God's Word is the same to a person, state, country, church, or anything else on the face of this earth. In any time-period, you wish to apply it in. It never changes. He said to preach it to every creature, how are we going to change that? Look how long the Jews have fought against receiving the truth. God's Word has declared it and anything formed against it cannot prosper, God has stated that and it is so.

I predicted the fall of this country when we elected Bill Clinton, and have stuck solidly with it ever since and watching it happening. Now you should be able to know about what I predicted when we elected Obama, especially the second time, it was no great surprise to me for God told me he was going to do it. I predicted just more of the same thing, for Obama was just another Carter and Clinton, combined and full of the Devil, on steroids. Operating over the bodies of Reagan and Bush whom the politicians, college professors, news reporters was finely able to slay in the eyes of the world and this country. By convincing this entire country that the credit cards were Reagan's fault that was maxed out under Bill Clinton's administration. With everybody carrying from five to twelve different credit cards in his pocket. With everybody living the most luxurious life under Clinton they had ever heard of, and blaming it on George W. Bush when he had to bail out the card holders. We fell into the most multiple records of bankruptcies that the world had ever seen; built up under Bill Clinton's administration.

While most of the country was living like millionaires, many of them were millionaires. Probably the biggest number of millionaires the world had ever seen, with a lot of the others living like it. Then in the big land slide election at the beginning of Bush's last two years after desperately trying to impeach Bush and trying to make the war effort fail, so they could impeach him, failed. Bush won the war despite their plans and efforts, but they did manage to fill the congress with Democrats promising to solve every problem, by printing and giving away more money. They were the problem for more debt on this country, under Obama, than all the presidents before Obama put together.

Nancy, still politicking and bragging, on her way into the congress to pick up her gavel, boasted that they had a sure plan to win back the white house in the next election. And they did; the federal banks that the Democrats had forced to make all them ridiculous loans, to keep the ridiculous promises that the ridiculous Democrats had been making for so many ridiculous years. Such as a home for every family, called the American dream (Maybe you have heard about it) and a two-car garage for every home, and two cars for every garage, and don't forget a chicken in every pot; women's rights to kill their babies, or marry another woman, or a horse if she chose. Thanks to California, New York, Hollywood, and Chicago; who must be some of Satan's favorite play grounds, they did all that she promised. I guess they thought we could furnish our own pot for the chicken, but more apt, just nobody ever asks them for one, for I'm sure they would have come up with a promise for a pot if they had. The stupid Republicans supporting them to get reelected got all the blame.

But the banks started crying that we had bailed out the card carriers but they didn't get back all their investments, all the late charges were not paid up, so the whole system was dumped on George. As I heard a few liberals call him, KING GEORGE, that was Nancy's plan. The whole finance system had collapsed and it was all and completely King George Bush's fault, he had done it all single handed, going around congress I suppose. He was about the only Republican left in DC, so it was bound to be his fault. (That must be where Obama learned that, you know he never learned such a dirty thing from the sparkling clean Democrats) so they worked their plan they had, putting the country in debt several trillion dollars. Nobody knows how many, the figure doesn't matter to them for they are not going to pay it off anyway. Mostly given to Obama's supporters to buy him and his constituents a career to a fortune and paid vacations and financing slaying the Republican party, from Lincoln until today.

The Democrats have a long memory. They are still chewing on the body of Lincoln every time it comes up, not so much to kill on it, they well took care of that. They just wanted to shift the credits and blame; changing history so to speak. The only thing that changed in history, was after the Civil War the Democrats moved to Washington and took over. But they are having a little trouble getting the bodies of Reagan and Bush buried and keeping them there. Their crime was in believing the Bible and the one true God. A death penalty, if the Democrat liberal news media are the judges, and they are.

So, you say where is the God that they believed in? I cannot show him to you for you are blind, just like Jesus said. But if you stay around long enough let me assure you he is going to show himself and you will know him. If you are seeing him for the first time it will be too late for you to do one thing about it, to prepare yourself.

I can assure you he is making ready; I cannot set dates because he has not set us one. Probably after you have seen many Christian's bodies lying before you and the ones remaining crying out for the God of Jacob, Isaac, and Abraham. He always answers when his people cries out in desperation. Do you see any Christians crying out to the living God in desperation? You will not see him till you do.

They used to be trying to get to this land of liberty to freely worship God. Do you think you could find any of that among them that are coming over our borders now? If they are trying to get here now for religious freedom it is not to worship the true God, but a false god. We do not have a freedom to worship the true God any more. Many are coming here now to kill Christians and vote Democrat, and will tell you so, to help the Democrats fully take over for them. Now *they* have a freedom of religion but Christians do not. We get the death penalty.

Obama and his Democrats and Hollywood, California and New York has done away with Christ and replaced him with a false god not caring what you call him. Just don't call him Jesus Christ, for that is not allowed. He is the Word of God, and dangerous to them. In other words, our government has outlawed the Bible and are trying to destroy you for preaching it.

Are you going to tell me that Christians voted for such a government as that? Trying, to impeach Bush, to put Rush Limbaugh in prison, to put fox news off the air, tried to have Glenn Beck committed for being crazy, putting pastors in jail for having a Christian school at their own expense. If it wasn't for the Catholic church, they would have closed all religious schools. The Catholic church could not afford that lick even though they have fully taken over our country, but they can hardly claim Christ. He doesn't fit at their head; the pope would have to step down. But no one cares if you close the schools that use the Bible, for that is Christianity. The Bible is Christ. Mystery Babylon don't need it and can never fit under our constitution or Bible, so they must go.

No, I do not believe that Christians voted for that government. I do not believe them voters know the God I do, and I do not care to know the god that they do. I do not care what denomination's book they have their names wrote down in. If you want my opinion I do not believe God cares either. He knows them, too.

I have never heard him mention looking for our names in any book but his. Called the "Lamb's Book of Life" and no one found in heaven or earth or under the earth, that could even take a peep upon it. Now remind me again how important that denominational book is, I'm sure apt to forget, if you don't keep reminding me.

They have succeeded in many things in their battle against Christianity, they got this country and most of the world to hate Bush, they put a God hating Muslim in the white house; got this country pretty much declared to be a Muslim country bowing to the Islam and honoring the Holy Koran (what Obama calls it) while dishonoring and outlawing the Bible to not have any place for existence. Have our government schools (Which is all of them that they put a dime into) teaching the Koran and Allah is the one god while Jesus is a fake and liar. A dangerous man whose name is not to be spoken in or near a government building or on any government grounds. Not even a silent prayer.

Congress passing and trying to pass laws that you can be put away for six years for offending a Muslim while they are swearing to kill all Christians and Jews and are working on it every day. You better not call a Muslim a terrorist for their Koran has constitutional protection, as a religious book. While it is taught in our schools as a culture. So, it is what it is, depending on where it is at, seems mighty convenient for the Islam and Democrats. Our Bible cannot find a crack anywhere in our system even to exist. It is too dangerous to be carried onto school property. It is dangerous to them, for it is not religion our government is afraid of, it is Jesus Christ which is the Bible and says so.

At the same time the Koran gets religious freedom protection and can be taught in our schools just by conveniently giving it two very pretty names. This is some of the name changing, or two names that I mentioned that our Democrats were so good at. I would like for our congressmen to explain a few things, but I'm a Christian and not allowed a voice in anything without denying my faith. If I get too sounding religious, I will be locked up.

I've had around three or four letters to the editor, that they ask for; refused to be printed in local small town newspapers. Either because they sounded too religious or it disagreed with their political views, the same thing. They are correct on one thing, if it is truth it is religious. All I give them was obvious facts and Biblical quotes. Where did they get the right to take my freedom of speech away? I believe I'd have more rights in Russia. I usually ask along about here, where are the Christians at? I still do not know. I am not so much complaining about the government and the people that are fighting for freedom from religion. Jesus said, we know what is in them and know what to expect to come out of them; from somebody that low life and trying to receive a little notoriety.

It is obvious how desperately hard up they are for craving a little notoriety from their God, the government. I just can't believe how many there is of them that just will not believe that the Bible is the Word of God, spiritually written and spiritually discerned, just like it says it is, and claiming to be a Christian? The Bible cuts the carnal completely out of it and leaves it with nothing in it to say.

I am compromising my writing a little, but not much, I believe I can find someone to print it for I believe every word I have written, and well know it is dangerous to tell truth.

After all, doesn't the world try to claim, and teach, that religion has caused all the wars on Earth? Truth is, it is the God haters and liar's religion that has caused the wars, call that a religion if you like for that is just what it is. The wars this country has fought are for my freedom to worship my one true God and speak and teach the Bible and truth, which is Jesus, and to protect our constitution. I believe I still have that right even though I know it is barely hanging on, and about the only country left to guarantee that right. They are hardly guarantying it anymore.

The carnal has nothing to add to the Spirit, is why God said for man to not add one word to his Word or diminish ought from one word in it. Man, can add all the words to his speaking and writing that he pleases, but Jesus said he would answer for every idle word. And when he speaks a Word of God, to make sure he can confirm it out of the mouth of two and three witnesses or it will not be God's word. That is sure to mean out of the mouth of spiritual witnesses. For God accepts no other. The Mystery Babylon Whore Church, that has taken over our country does not believe in the Spirit of Christ. Jesus said he did not need the testimonial of a man, he knows everything in man. The truth is man has stooped so low for his flesh, to sell his soul for a little pocket change, and a flash of self-glory; what a pity? All flesh is carnal, and cannot add one thing to the Spirit.

No, government is not afraid of religion; they are the most religious thing on earth. Government is an establishment of religion. Our constitution says they cannot pass a law favoring a religion. I believe about every person on earth has his own religion. It is simply what he believes and puts his trust in, is his religion. The Mystery Babylon religious beast rider, that has taken our country, has lost two world wars to the Bible, which is Jesus Christ. The Bible is what they are scared to death of, not our religion. Their religion killed over a hundred-million Christians for teaching the Bible. Their religion is filled with blasphemy and drunk on the blood of the saints and martyrs of Jesus Christ. Their religion has the blood of prophets and saints and all that has been slain on the earth on their hands.

Christ is going to reveal it to the world when he destroys her in one days' time and lets the world watch it at a distance. Afraid to get close for the fear of her smoke and torment. Her judgment comes in one hour. Read about it in the book of revelations.

Jesus is truth, him and his disciples died for it. And has said we are no better than them. And he is going to avenge the blood of the earth on Mystery Babylon. The Bible is the only writings we have that has the seal of Jesus Christ, backed by his disciples, that we used to swear over it, the truth, the whole truth, nothing but the truth. Before we became so smart we out grew God. Qualifying ourselves to correct God, and tell everybody the way God should have said it and should have wrote it. And should have designed this great creation. My goodness, things have changed in my seventy-five years. We come a long way baby. And love to tell our children about it. Jesus said what have you gained if you gain the world and lose your soul? We are not as quick to tell our children about that.

We are going strong but I believe we better check with our navigator. And double check the direction we are going in. You can't be going south and end up north without going over the south, around the world, then back toward north. That's a lot of traveling just because one would not start out in the right direction to start with. Just hope you can last that long. Once again carnal is backwards to truth, the Spirit is always right and real, no manner what it appears like to us. God is going to prove it. Don't be caught on the wrong side when he does. Jesus said today is the day of salvation, and we are not promised a tomorrow. Jesus is all truth, and all truth is Jesus Christ and is the only thing that can and will always set you free, if you will walk in him. Of course, the carnal cannot see freedom as the Spirit does. As it sees no word the same. Therefore, it is called a new creature and born again. I would recommend anyone to try it, but the flesh is to die out. God is a Spirit, and is constantly at war with the flesh.

CHAPTER 8

A HOUSE DIVIDED CANNOT STAND

Taking the spirit out of something is turning it over to carnality. Then allowing each person to have his own interpretation to fit his own taste and will tell you so in a moment's time. It is just not so with God's Word. You cannot take the spirit out of the Spirit; this is the cause of so many division and separations in the body of Christ. Without the Bible, which is the Spirit, I would not know one way to get two people to come together as one in the favor of God.

That is why God's Word says there is just no way for a non-believer to make it into the Kingdom of God. Without the Spirit, God's Word, God's people are divided. Anything of another spirit will react to his own, selfish, jealous, lustful, desires, to deny someone else of their God given rights. Even when it is not taking one thing from himself and is plainly not one bit of his business. But for no reason he is determined to deny everyone else of their rights.

I cannot tell you why, but I can tell you why the flesh, or self, is intolerant to the Spirit of God. God told us to be quite to mind our own business. Since self hears everything backwards to God, it thought he said to mind everybody's business but our own.

God has laid man out in two categories, the ones that have the Spirit of God are his, and the ones that do not are none of his. This is where the division is at. As I have said, man has a strong incline to see what he wants to see, hear and believe just what he wants to hear and believe. Sometimes, regardless of what has been said. This is God's very words. People think they know who is saved and who is not when they do not know the Spirit of God and could not recognize a lie if they were hit over the head with one. Reason being they do not want to. You have heard the old saying, "Truth hurts," even though not much in these last generations. I can assure you, it still hurts the heck out of lies and perversion and flesh. God will not accept one part of a lie. You may, but truth will not. That house will not ever stand.

The Bible says a bunch about people who cannot love the brethren. One of them that is said in a few different ways, is he has not passed from death unto life and is walking in darkness still. Or in other words he is a zombie. Without God's Spirit, he is none of God's. I believe that eliminates him from walking in the Spirit of God. I don't have to judge nobody to say that the people that are Christians are mighty few because the Bible tells us that, over and over. And when I look at the divisions in the body of Christ I know plainly, what the biggest reason on earth is, for so many to not make it into the Kingdom of God. They cannot accept Truth when it has been handed straight to them. Not here on earth, nor when Jesus comes back to get the ones that is his. While billions are going to be left behind crying and screaming only a very few is going to be chosen. The odds are going to be very high against any man. *The fear of the Lord* is one of the most demanded things to being a child of God. It is the beginning of knowledge and the beginning of wisdom, and the foundation to build anything solid on.

If you don't have a fear of the lord, God says you don't know anything toward him. Just a carnal mind, we are told, knows nothing about the Spirit of God. We are told to read these things in the Bible and judge ourselves. Any man that can read and know that they are in the Bible and not fill a little fear of God I believe that man is more than probably crossed the line, hard hearted, stiff necked, no conscience of his own sins. Guilty of many other things the Bible names, and the Spirit of God can never draw him to the Lord Jesus Christ. If he cannot be broken up in his own spirit he will be one among the billions that will be left behind, just that simple, not one among the few that will be chosen.

Just for a little clarification in the way I have been stating a few facts here, don't amount to anything unless someone wants to be a little contentious. But the fact is plain in the Bible that Jesus is not coming for taking anybody out and others be left behind. Jesus is coming back to join them that are his, to set up an everlasting kingdom on, the heaven and earth. The others will be taken out, with the old heaven and earth, and the ones whose names are not found written in the Lamb's Book of Life, and thrown into the eternal lake of fire. Only then is the new heaven and earth spoke of, appearing as coming down, not as us going up. We have just heard it preached that way so long and hard, we just sort of automatically express in that way, but it is not recorded in the Bible that way.

That should not be too hard to see if we will look just a little for our self, instead of turning to a brother and commenting how "That preacher don't know nothing about what he is talking about" and stomping out the door. There is not one ounce of fear of God in that man, whether the preacher knew what he was talking about are not. "I've had it happen to me," God says he hates any man that sows discord among the brethren.

If your instrument is out of tune in God's house I believe you should just keep it quiet, for God hates someone that sows any discord among his brethren. Only someone that has no fear of God or no beginning of knowledge would dare do something like that. Disagreement and discord causes division and should never be handled blatantly in the middle of a service. A house divided cannot stand, Jesus has told us for two thousand years.

I am trying to get into a little of how easy it is to get out of the Spirit of God. Any amount of separating or dividing in the-midst of the Spirit of God is too much. It is like a weapon for Satan to use against the unity of the Body of Christ that Jesus has called us into, members one of another. Only them that are in and of the Spirit of God can understand that. It is from the Word of God that was written by the Spirit of God, man did not write one word in it. Even though the world wants to give King James or someone else the credit. God says different, says it was spiritually written and spiritually discerned. Now which one do you want to believe and teach for?

Any amount of calling the Bible wrong is blasphemy. Jesus made it very plain that it is the worst sin that a man can commit. Jesus said plainly that it was the only sin that would not ever be forgiven. People get divided over that scripture about as much as any of the scriptures. They do not understand it. No marvel there, for carnal does not understand any scripture without help from the Spirit, which is the giver of all knowledge. Therefore, blaspheme cannot be forgiven.

You cannot be forgiven by the Spirit disagreeing with the Spirit and refusing to believe. It is not a one-time act that you cannot undo. Like everything else with God, it is a heart and mind condition not an act. Are you expected to undo all the other sin acts you committed? No, but you are told to repent and get them out of your heart and mind. If you don't they will destroy you, for God will not forgive you for them either, if you still have blaspheme. It is not the people you have sinned against, it is the sin you cannot get forgiveness for any sin, while still doing it. This is where vengeance and restitution comes in to play. They are two more different subjects. I have settled the blaspheme issue in my mind by simply saying, blaspheme is a sin that cannot be forgiven, you just must quit and get out of it or better yet, get it out of you.

But, if you can prove someone misused a privilege and caused you some damage or hindrance, then let them order him to make it right from the evidence and facts presented about that particular-situation. But not making it a law just to see someone with a similar belief that he is guilty of the same crime and gets the same punishment. How can one undo blaspheme except just get it out of himself. What I'm saying is, men have taken common sense out of the law and everything else. When you throw out the Bible and Truth, it makes every man for himself overnight, and that is what we have now and causes division and separations and raises a few thousand denominations. Then they are powerless. This is what blaspheme does. Therefore, God hates any amount of it and will not tolerate very much of it among his people.

I cannot judge, and will never attempt to, but it is true, that many a highly religious people are on their way to hell.

In judging and enforcing man's laws they have taken out common sense and God's laws. When it comes to God's laws and common sense I am ready to stand on my rights to my hurt. If we had more Christians that could just muster up a little courage to stand up for himself and help his fellow man a little like Jesus said, even just occasionally. I'm sure it would help in preserving a few of our rights.

And might even gain us a little respect from them people that think we are stupid trash under their feet. And deserving of no respect because we will not stand up for our God and worship their god instead. If we are not going to demand a little respect, then it is for sure we will receive less and less. Respect is required to be earned. I'll stand up for a weaker person much quicker than I will for myself. It flat turns me off to see people do the opposite for personal gain, and I've seen a bunch.

It seems like a little in almost everybody around me. It is not that I'm right or you're right, it is just both of us acknowledging that God is always right, and man is a liar. That is just what he says, and I believe him. Once again, the Bible is the only thing to settle a dispute. They like to quote our Bible to us, "Thou shalt not kill." I can tell them they are taking it out of context, with no understanding about them. And not establishing every word as God has commanded us to.

They can find no establishing scriptures for the way they are quoting the word kill. I can find a small text of Bible, establishing it the way it is meant. First off, how many places can you find where God allowed his people to kill? How many places in scriptures did he ordered them to kill?

Even down to everything that breathed, women, children, old and young, even their animals. One place he said to dash their children's heads against a stone.

Show me the place where God repented and grew soft on the flesh, or carnality. If you are going to throw Christ and the New Testament into the picture here, Christ is the complete Word of God. Maybe you should read a little of what he said and did. He not only wrote the old and new testament; he is every word of it. Unless you want to call it a lie. Who killed Ananias and Sapphira for lying to the Holy Ghost in the book of acts? What about the scripture that God said, don't you kindle my anger just a little, I might just snitch you from the earth?

Yes, he said the government is on his shoulders now. But where did he change the scriptures and issue a discharged for the people under him that is his government over every government of the world, of which Solomon said there is no discharge. How many places did he refer to his people as a standing army and putting on and wearing the armor for the battle we are in. Whether you know it or not, we are in a battle and there are causalities. If God's people would fight Satin's people as hard as they will fight one another, Satan would not stand a chance. And yes, God has said there is a time to kill and a time to make alive. I do not believe Jesus would command any man to kill, if he did not have it in him, but you better be real close to him if you want him to kill for you.

And to keep going the way we are going is going to run Christians out of any rights at all if we keep agreeing with God haters and voting for them, and fighting among ourselves. God is the only answer and as far as I know, man has not come up with any more an appropriate name for him than the one he gave Moses when he asks "Who shall I say sent me?" Our only side to get on, is God's side, the great, I Am.

Maybe it doesn't matter with you what his name is, but I will promise you it does with God. How many people do you know that it doesn't matter to them what you call them? It's a very good way to get punched in the nose almost anywhere you are at. I would assume, if you don't want to get punched in the nose by God, maybe you should watch what you call him. He said to fear him. He is a terrible God, he is a vengeful God, he is a consuming fire, and many other things. You can read all about him in that Bible you refuse to believe. It is living dangerously to not study and believe it. When you speak against or wrongly about him, that is called blaspheme in God's book.

I verily know I am to keep the faith and to do everything in and for the glory of God, and if he told me not to do something, I hope I would be able to stop. But I feel a lot of leeway for self-defense and to protect them that I am responsible for. Under certain circumstances I would kill if God did not intervene. He has a few times.

You don't have to fear a false god he is powerless to lay a hand on you, you can call him anything you want to, he just does not exist. Only the crazy people that think he does and they are working for him and will be promised a reward of carnal things in the hereafter, even for killing you. How is he going to collect his carnal reward in the hereafter when nothing carnal is going to make it there? A false god is only in your imagination, and can give no rewards, people do that. Not many of them are going to be in the hereafter.

Kill, is a very broad word, comes in many ways and many forms covering a lot of territory and a lot of things.

I believe you would need to read a lot of other Bible to confirm its usage anywhere it is used in the Bible by the way it is used, and you can find conformation. If you want to see it as most people preach it, then congress had better never kill a bill, and you better never kill a glass of milk, and don't swat a fly. The battle is in your mind, and common sense. Get your mind right.

Isaiah said of our times, "Truth is fallen in the streets; we are turned around backwards, calling evil good and good evil. Anybody that dares to speak truth makes himself a prey." How can the so-called Christians not see and recognize this when it is told to us so plain in Isaiah, for the last days? It seems our preachers must not know how to read or don't know how to preach truth anymore. Maybe they are afraid of making themselves a prey.

It's for sure that there is a slim few that are preaching the Bible as Truth or as the absolute Word of God and nothing else is. If they do not believe that it is, then they do not believe the Bible. That makes me want to ask, what they are preaching out of? Do they think the Holy Ghost does not believe the Bible it wrote? It seems they must be preaching out of that Mother of Harlots and Abominations Church, told about in the seventeenth chapter of Revelations that covers the world over. I think that is a big church. That was drunk on the blood of the saints they killed, for preaching from the Bible. Yes, they believed the Bible was a powerful weapon like it said it was and is. They also thought that they were setting in God's seat and could use it against any of their enemies or anything that disagreed with them, so they did. They became the church told about, starting the explanation in the sixteenth chapter of Revelations. Holding the only Bible there was and the power that went along with it, if no one else could look upon it, how was they going to be exposed? God's word says, how can they believe when they have not heard? How can they hear without a preacher? How can he preach least he be sent?

When King James authorized the Bible to be written by the Spirit of God, England took it up and started teaching it, the beast's power was broken up, driven into perdition. The world was led out of the dark ages. At least God's people was led out of a control that was influenced heavy by that rider of the beast that was the biggest slaying machine of God's people that has ever been built on the face of the earth, even until today. Becoming the Mystery Babylon Whore Church, with control of the beast trying to restore the beast's power over the earth.

Its killing has been stopped by America in two world wars for a season but the beast, that is in perdition, and its rider has never given up retaining their power back again and have sworn and told us just exactly how they were going to do it. "Become imbedded in our colleges and teach our Bible out." Have you noticed how scarce our Bible is getting in our schools? Satan knows the Bible is the only enemy he is afraid of. He has mankind worshiping his seat in the north parts above God like he said he would do. All he needs to do is kill Christ, which is the Bible now, and he would have God defeated. The Jews must cry out to Christ to give Christ the right to kill Satan, the Antichrist, and the False Prophet of the Mystery Babylon Whore Church.

They said, when they start turning out our doctors, lawyers and teachers, what would there be left? Then they would have the control back again. They have been doing that lately at an alarming rate. God is having to raise up ten kingdoms in the Middle East, ruled by the Antichrist, to eat the scattered Christians first, from the Mystery Babylon beast rider at Rome. Undoubtable some good ones are falling; for the Antichrist, cannot tell, nor does he care, about the difference between the hypocritical and the true Christians. God is to send an angel through the air to warn his people to come out of her before it burns the city itself, clean from the earth. I do not know what form the angel will be in but I bet only God's people will see him to know him, and that will be the ones that are looking for him. I have a strong feeling he is already flying; and it is looking like only a few is going to hear him. He will be a spirit, you know, and he will be speaking a spiritual language. The Antichrist and False Prophet spirits have been killing lately to an alarming rate to any Christian that it comes across. God is raising up the Antichrist Kingdom in the Middle East to keep the Babylon Whore from completely taking over America.

They will try to unite, and will for a while. But God will turn them against each other. The Whore will be burned from the earth. We are too weak and spiritless to protect our self and we do not have a Godly kingdom any more.

I have been telling this story mostly from history but the Bible tells it the very same way. The Bible concludes the very end plainly, but history has not covered the end of it yet but is coming very close upon it. The very end of time, as told from the Bible, will be very short.

I believe the reason it is so difficult for carnal man to write it into a book, and explain it very well, is, man just cannot write it as cruel as it is going to be and make it sound believable. Here is just a *few* things, God has said about it. That the whole world has been polluted and corrupted by people, so bad, he is going to burn the whole thing up. Christians can expect persecution from everywhere in the world. A beast is carnal man power without God. The Bible teaches that man without God is a beast, or animal. It will get so bad that men of all ranks will go into the caves of rocks and try to commit suicide and pray for the rocks to fall on them to hide them from the face of the one on the thrown. Death will flee from them. God, will scorch them with the sun, most of them will not repent, but curse God instead. The angles with the seven vials of the wrath of God, poured one of them on the kingdom of the beast, it went into full darkness and men gnawed their tongues for pain. A star falls from heaven and burns one third of the earth. Great hail fell from heaven mixed with fire and blood, is just a few of the weird things that were happening. Now show me somebody that can fully visualize a few dozens of these things and explain them to men where he can fully understand them. Divisions in God's people are the cause of all the failures in Christ's body, a house divided cannot stand, can nobody hear Christ's Words? Somebody back in history said the words "United we stand, divided we fall." We've about forgot that one too.

I've seen several churches with a board hanging up on the wall, inside front of the church. Facing the congregation, with a list of things wrote in black letters big enough to be read from the back row saying, "This is what this church believes." I wonder why they couldn't just say we believe and teach the Bible and have a much smaller board and less paint? Just saying what could unite them; instead of naming the things that would divide them from other Christians. You can see the ones they are proud of when they have them listed, the ones that divides.

I know their answer, "The Bible can have so many different interpretations it is not possible to tolerate any others." "If we cannot bend enough to come together as one, we will never be one." Is that not saying, our church is the one? I'm saying the Bible is the one, the only one. Church is the house of God for his people to come together as one to reason with God. God cannot reason with a divided bunch of people, with each, and every man thinking he is the one that is right.

Did not God say that every man is right in his own eyes? If they will not hear truth, how will you ever bring them together?

Blaspheme is, *speaking against,* you can never be one with truth, speaking against truth. Please allow me to tell you a very big fact, or truth, whatever you want to call it, right here. Allow me to catch my breath and I'll start into it.

First, let me explain, if you bend a little, and they bend a little, you are both going to be crooked. I read of no place in God's Kingdom for crooked people. That includes Hillary. God speaks in the book of Amos of a plumb line, that implies straight. He was referring to the Bible being as a plumb line that he was going to give us to set us up straight by. Which we are to refer everything to, if you want to get them, or yourself straight, there is nothing else that qualifies. The Bible is plain it is Jesus Christ, the Word of God, the life of anything that has life, and a few other claims. The Bible says to establish every word of God by the mouth of two and three witnesses, plus you can look for the example. The Bible is the place he is talking about to look, I am sure. You can confirm that in maybe a few dozen places.

If the scripture they are trying to preach is correctly quoted, you will find it very little trouble to find your conformations and your examples. If you can't find them, you need to have a Pastor that can help you. If you cannot find a scripture that can prove it right, then you can find one that can prove it wrong. If you look long enough you can find one or the other for sure. You should never listen to a preacher that teaches a scripture to call another scripture a lie, this is just not so. The way one of them is quoted and misunderstood is what is wrong.

There is a danger in lack of understanding and some needs help badly. Some of them are at some high and honorable places. But the same rules apply right from the Bible. This is what the Bible teaches, the carnal and the Spirit cannot mix. The carnal is deaf and blind and void of any understanding of the Spirit, and does not know one thing about the Spirit of God. Backed up in maybe a dozen or two places. Just to think carnally is sure death.

Any religion that will not accept the new birth into the Spirit is a dead religion. Only alive carnally and only has any power that it can muster up under its own steam; and the steam it can get from men that will align up with it. That is all the power and effect it can have and will not prosper if it goes against God. It will be burned up or destroyed if it gets in God's way of performing his word. I know that is going to bring up a lot of questions in anyone's mind that is listening to this with any interest, and it should. I do not have the space in this book to answer them all, but can tell you that the Bible has every answer. That is why you need a good Pastor, one that can answer them for you instead of just tearing down the source that you got them from. You can know if your pastor starts out that way it means he has not studied his Bible enough to explain the answer of your question to you. There is much difference in talking about a source, or talking to a source, or person. The Spirit of God will build you up, not tear you down, or anything else that is not present. That is what I meant by the difference between talking to someone and talking about someone. It only destroys the things that come against it, like a contrary spirit. If he does not have you an answer, you should have the right to expect him to get you an answer, which is his job. If you are wrong the answer will straighten you out. What profit would you or he gain if he was to just tear your source of knowledge down completely to the ground, if he did not answer your question? Just steers you away from it or tries to have it killed.

Those are the spirits of human nature if you don't like the message, kill the messenger, that is what they did to the prophets, Jesus, and his disciples, even of today. And tried to do it to Moses and Aaron. And is what the beast riding church at Rome did to be drunk on the blood of the saints and the martyrs of Jesus Christ. Killing over one hundred million of them, to print, preach and possess the only Bible left after Constantine burned all the paper and history that he could get his hands on. {If you are thinking, I should forgive and forget; read the 17th 18th and 19th chapters of Revelations and see how Jesus is going to handle it, when it comes up in God's remembrance. Then we can talk about it some more.} They were trying to wipe out any record of Jesus Christ; but what *they* were telling the world. This is the starting of the Mother Church and the plus thousand years of slaughtering of God's people.

If we had more preachers that believed the Bible and knew how to study it like it says to; they could sure solve a lot of problems instead of causing more. We would not need a few thousand denominations to divide us, just "one" to preach the Bible to unite us if they would use the Bible correctly.

It is the only qualifying instrument in the world that could accomplish this. Parents might remember, at this point, that they are the Pastor to that family that they brought fourth. The Bible would work, for God would destroy the unbelievers out from among the believers. This is the way he has done it from the beginning. We would not have to hang a sign in the pulpit to get them to leave or to have an excuse to throw them out. God could handle that if his spirit is present with liberty and unity. If Jesus had not come down for us, there would not be one human being saved. He did come down and is going to save a few chosen ones, only a few. We all have a chance to be one of them, by accepting his Spirit and denying the flesh.

The Bible is his Spirit, he said so. Work and build toward the future instead of working and building to the present and self, which will disappear when God breathes on it. You are not called to worry about and tear down anything the Devil is building. Just follow Jesus, that is his job. It is an easier way, just hard on the flesh. Jesus told and showed us that it had to die, and it will. Our spirit and soul does not have to die with it. If we make the right choses in this life.

There is some that live out a long miserable life, trying to keep this fleshly body happy and content. They will never attain that. Most of them will lose their souls trying, especially if they succeed at all. A few others may save their souls but are going to find they didn't lay up one piece of treasure for themselves in eternity. Nothing they laid up or enjoyed down here is going to be taken with them.

Our government is still of the people, isn't it? I believe the People have been divided and conquered by Mystery Babylon, and Allah and Islam's religion just like the Bible warned against. I'm positive our government has, being of the people instead of being of Christ as he said it should be. Being of the people worked out well, when the people were of God. I challenge you to check the number one religion in Washington today. All of them have been to college and been schooled by that beast rider's government schools. Why do all the selfish, greedy, power hungry government people; and their constituents that have sold their souls for a piece of the power and money that is in running this country; hate the Bible as the biggest enemy in the world?

Because it is the biggest enemy in the world that evil has, and the best friend and weapon that a righteous person will ever have. It is the truth and power of Jesus Christ all in one, and will not ever suffer defeat. Do you finally see why Washington DC and all the other Devil worshipers want to kill it, they hate it? The Devil was the one that suffered defeat at Calvary, not Christ. The Devil is telling his people, which is backwards to the Spirit, that he won. And those that are seeing backwards believe him. Just another lie that God will turn them over to because that is what they want to believe.

Let me see if I can dwell on the word power and authority for just a while. It seems to be what religion is mostly about. It seems to be what politics and government is all about. It seems to be what about anything moving is all about. Maybe everybody ought to be a little bit ready to talk about it some. Reckon we could develop a little unity if we could all be pulled a little closer together? I have been writing that it is what God has called us into, even into one body. I do not like the word, but I believe the carnal calls it a religion; and tries to blame every problem man has on somebody else's religion. Of course, each man thinks his religion is the only one that is right. Does not God say that every man is right in his own eyes?

Right now, we are in the process of voting on the president for this great country, most people think it is the highest office of power in the world. We have rioting and burning of our cities, killing of our peace keepers, illegals invading our southern borders and saying they are going to kill us and fly their flag over our white house. Going across our country doing it. Our federal judges passing laws saying that it is a right they have. For them to burn our flag in public and just call it a speech and we must protect them while they do it. Seems like our president don't know a thing to do but fan the flames.

Reckon he is not only stupid and blind but maybe he has a wrong religion about him? Does he not know that he oversees all our military and could stop them Devil possessed radicals from killing our police, burning up their cars and our city's businesses. If he cannot whip a crowd of rioters and arrest them overseeing our whole army, what would he do if another country attacks us? Of course, all a Democrat can preach is meet them with flowers and nobody will get hurt, was McGovern's words. Carter looking for a table to sit down and sign anything they wanted signed. Clinton trying to sell everything we own, even down to our souls. Obama thinks we need to increase our money printing machines, they cannot keep up, is the problem. He has brought nothing but peace since he has been in office and we are so much better off he cannot find enough words to tell us how much. And puts all the praise on himself that he thinks he deserves. I don't happen to think like him. But I don't say he needs to be impeached, just took out on the white house lawn and hung, would suffice.

I am sure you are thinking I am talking crazy, then I think it is time we looked for a crazy person to put in as our president. I can't imagine him doing any worse than the one we have. I would be for suggesting a head shrink for anybody that voted for him, -and two times??!! It is probably too late for them.

It takes unity for a house to stand and it takes some one that cares about the house to lead it. And I reckon we should look for someone that cares about America's house, to vote for. Instead of a hypocrite and liar that cares only for self and power. God hates selfish liars.

I say there will not be one person in heaven with a sore arm where God twisted it to get him to come along, it just won't be. Satan uses no morals or ethics in his methods. God has given each one of us a complete free will to make our own choice. Even to the choice of training our kids the way we want to raise them and told us they will go in the way we train them to go. How could he do it any other way and say he gave us the kids. God and one can make a majority.

We have at least two examples in the Bible where God called a kid home because he knew he wasn't going to be raised in a right and just way as the kid deserved. In other words, he didn't have a chance. He told us plainly he would hold us responsible, but we want to blame God for all our failings and the way the kids turn out. Can you explain to yourself how you are going to work that out? How are we going to justify ourselves? How are we going to hold God accountable? I sure can't, and believe me I have been trying, maybe somebody can help me out there a little bit. Again, I say if we refuse to study and believe the Bible we are lost. It should be our guide in everything.

Maybe we could seek out some of the hundreds and hundreds of denominations that have succeeded in dividing the Christians apart from truth, the Bible, the true God, the real God, all the same thing. And try to find and understand what led them to a false god of many names that has conquered them by dividing. Lying to them with lying promises that they want to hear and believe. Now you should see why Jesus said for us to confess. Probably not a one of them will admit he is wrong, does not know he is lost, and will not believe that the Bible is Jesus Christ like it says it is.

In other words, he will not believe the Bible, how does he know what to confess; or who to confess to. What are you going to get him saved to? Seventy-two virgins and all the dope he wants through all eternity, with a god that orders anything killed that disagrees with him. Even to teaching them they have-to believe like him or they will be killed and they will have-to kill anybody that does not believe like him. The big difference in hell here on earth and hell in eternity; is hell in eternity will not have the comfort of death or dope.

I ask in one of my books, what did the virgins get? One Man for each seventy-two virgins? And all the dope she can eat. Is that what the mother church of Revelations taught and showed the world, before God moved on King James of England. To have them that dared, to write a Bible to lead us out of literal captivity and sure death. For them that dared to read, believe and teach it.

God made England the most powerful little island in the entire world, because they had the Bible and stood up for it. He made the English language, the leading language of the world and started running the world by it. The world church fought harder to try to destroy the Bible than they did to destroy the church that Jesus and his Apostles started when he was walking on this earth. The church only had the *anointing* of the Spirit, the Bible *is* the Spirit, they had *it.*

Nothing could stand up to England until they started to try to set in the seat of God; and tried to run God's church from the government. Just like the church they come out of that was killing Christians as fast as they could catch them. And run the Christians out of the country, which they did. But they took their Bible with them. They come to America, not for gold, not for furs, not for the fountain of youth; but for the liberty to worship God, the God of the Bible. Not a god of the heathen or paganism, but the God of the Bible, the Lord Jesus Christ.

The God of that Bible they carried owned the gold, the furs, the fountain of youth and everything else you can think of, he owns that too. God allowed them to start the building of the greatest nation ever built on the face of this earth. They suffered many trials and battles, made mistakes as God said they would. But the Christians used to think this great country, with its God given liberties and wealth; was worth every bit of it.

Satan took over our schools and taught us we had no liberty, spirit or riches, except what the government chooses to give us. Even taught us we could not eat well unless we prayed to the government. And proved it to us by telling us like little children to bury our faces in our arms, on our school desk and pray to God for a bar of candy to be put on their desk. When they had them to look up, there was no bar of candy. Then they were told to bury their faces again and pray to the "government" this time, for a bar of candy. While their faces were buried, they walked around through the seats and placed a bar of candy on each desk. YEAA the good old government always comes through, so there goes all good old God fearing America's faith out the door. You can always depend on them smart politicians, they will not ever let you down. Just pay your taxes and vote for the ones that promises you the most candy. If they can get enough of our money and votes, they will always have you a candy bar, even if they must get China to take a mortgage on our country, no problem. God is ending up with a lot of spoiled, candy-eating kids; with bad teeth.

If you don't believe that my God is still in charge of this earth; just crawl under the porch and watch. Just don't die while you are under the porch. You will see the next big event shaping up to come upon this world. It would be a shame to be asleep and miss it. If you have a preacher worth two-cents, he should be telling you something about it now. And don't let the God haters cut off his head.

If that is not a fact from the Bible, then just send me on up to join Jesus and the rest of his disciples. I will soon be seventy-five years old and do not have much time left to lose, either way. Everything to gain, I almost welcome it. You need not give me too much credit for being brave, just level headed. I know the side of my bread that has the butter on it, the upper side, of course. Tell your preacher, the Bible is the butter. Maybe he can take a hint, but help to protect his head for him. Vote for somebody beside a headhunter, you might help save a lot of heads from being cut off. Might even decide it is not so bad to have a Christian involve in politics, if you can learn to recognize one. It will be one that is not busy cutting off heads, might be a start. And one that is not fighting with every other Christian around him; and is content with the Jesus he has. Will be a good start. He will not be blaspheming the Bible, for sure.

CHAPTER 9

JOIN OR DIE

This slogan was drawn up for the thirteen colonies. It was displayed in the form of a joint-snake. A call for them to come together as God had called them, or divided they would die as Jesus said.

Let me tell a little story here, this one is a story. When I was just a kid I thought, a joint snake was just a myth until one day I was walking to the barn on a narrow trail through the weeds. Just coming up to the barn, and stepped on a joint snake. He flew apart all over the place just like they said. I could not find the piece that had his head on it, to kill him. So being told that they had to get back together or they would die, I just thought, I'll fix his wagon. So, I just picked up a middle piece and slung it well upon the tin barn roof, said that will take care of you and went on.

Next day I was walking along that same path and behold, there was that snake lying there again; looking like he was doing fine? I wondered how he had got on top of the barn to get the joint to join himself back up. Looking a little closer, he had joined himself up on a corncob, looking fine. It's hard to stop a serpent. You need to cut off his head.

Satan is a copier, cannot create anything but can change the meaning of anything if he can get his hands on it if you don't cut off his head. He has been using the word, pictured with an entirely different meaning, with the beast riding church at Rome since around three hundred AD. Meaning to join their church are they would kill you. And they did, killed tens and tens of millions before the Bible got successfully completed and preached, and led the world out of the dark ages. It could only do that when preached from the Spirit of God. And separated from all the pieces of Bibles and different denominations that had the world so confused and were cutting off each other's head.

Satan saw within a three-hundred-year period after they slew the Lord Jesus Christ, the more he tried to kill his influence the more it grew. Kind of like a wild fire, the harder he stomped, the more it spread. So, he joined the church through the emperor, Constantine, and thinks he has been running it since. And well did, until the Bible was written in answer to the prayer from Tyndale as he was being burned at the steak. By the great whore church of Revelations; the beast rider; drunk on the blood of the saints. For doing some great work toward writing a genuine Bible. He was using some writings of Wycliffe and some other great men of God that was trying to write a complete authenticated Spiritual book.

The ruling church of the day got so mad at the influence of Wycliffe; who had died and escaped the death at the stake, on top of a burning brush pile. But, his writings were becoming more influential. They dug up his bones, burned them and spread them out into a stream of water to disappear. I reckon thinking they would kill his influence for good. They are still trying to kill his influence, just like they are trying to do to Jesus Christ. Guess that is why Jesus took his bones with him when he was resurrected, didn't want the satanic beast rider to be burning them and casting them into a brook, or upon a barn roof.

God said the prayers of a righteous man availeth much. I wonder what part of all the killings, did they think would be a favor to God? Jesus told his disciples they would be putting them to death thinking they were doing God a favor. All of them they put to death, I guess. It is not the Bible that I do not understand; it is the devil possessed people, that cut off heads and burn up people while they are still alive. They have a weird way of thinking. And have no excuse whatsoever to believe the Devil and follow him except to believe and love his lying promises to their lust craving carnal flesh without the Spirit of God. When a complete dummy should know that they are a lie.

Our Democrat Party, being completely radicalized (Devil possessed) has been taken over by Satan, whichever way you say it; and is on the verge of selling our country into hell. It is Satan's only plan. If Hillary is elected, our Supreme Court is gone. It has been on just about the last straw of hope for some time now and may have cost Justice Scalia his life for protecting it. Your head will be in literal danger if you go against the Democrats in any way. Many people have lost their life mysteriously without any explanation, during and since the Clinton administration. Many lies and facts have been coming out of them ever since but anyone should know a Democrat is never held accountable by our set up system. Why should they? The Democrats set it up.

I am sure they have an unwritten law hid some place that says a Democrat, above a certain rank, cannot be held accountable. I wish I could find it but I have not been able to. I'd like to look in under the Supreme Court's bench, or the Lame Stream Media's desk but I am sure I will never get the permission. I do not have a pair of them Democrat's rose colored glasses that they seem to have put on most of our country. But I believe I can read it from down here in Arkansas; written in the clouds.

I heard someone just a few days ago, refer to ABC, CBS, NBC, CNN and a few more as being news reporters. They sure have had me fooled for some time. I was thinking they were left headed Liberal Democrat's and queers and atheist and headhunter's campaign headquarters. Just shows you how little I know about what is going on. I have watched the federal judges go so far left they have run off the map and cannot be measured any more. But that doesn't mean you cannot hear from them. The FBI has just announced they cannot find enough evidence to recommend charges for Hillary. I don't know why; they are both living in the same shack together out left somewhere. They read about two pages of them to the public they found somewhere. Where did they go to law school at? Hillary's free international school that she has promised us?

I am so old and have severe arthritis, so bad I cannot turn my neck, my eyes and ears are about gone, but sometimes I feel like that may be my blessing. Especially when I cannot look to the left, or hear the lame stream news media on TV. So, I just don't look to the left or TV very much, when I am looking to where I want to go.

I study and preach God's word and cannot see anything but hell to go to when I look in their direction. I am told the right way to go is straight, forward, narrow, and up, not easy to attain for you can get off on the right or the left. I am not brave enough to argue with God. I read in the old testament, where a bunch of people were swallowed up by the earth into a lake of fire, when trying to argue with God; them, their families and all their belongings. Another group was led around in the wilderness for forty years and died there, within three days of the promised land for arguing with God.

God said that old law was there for our learning and example, that we should know what to do and know what not to do. As I say often, I happen to believe the Word of God. He said he wrote it; he cannot lie. And promised the same reward for anyone telling a lie, making a lie, helping a lie, believing a lie, or loving a lie. Said he hates all liars. No lie will stand up to a truth and nothing backs up a lie but another lie.

Ever get the feeling God does not like a lie? Where does that leave the politicians, the TV personalities, the college professors? Watch any advertising you see on TV; it is hard to see how them people sleep at night. Boy, I am glad I do not have one thing to do with judging anyone of them. The one I have a hard time getting over; remember how an Anacin Aspirin tablet could take a hard knot out of a tight piece of rope? And it would fix your headache. Very impressive, wouldn't you think?

God said if you give God-speed to an evil person you will be partaker of his evil deeds. Lying is evil. I quoted that for the ones that are asking why I think any of this is any of my business. I like to know the spirit of anything I must deal with in any way, that is my business, and should be yours. God said if a person came to you bringing any other gospel but Jesus Christ and he crucified, to not let him into your house. And many other like things he said. A lot of people need to study their Bible.

If I was asked to name, the biggest liar over the world I would be at odds to say. Hillary is the biggest liar but Obama is the most convincing and successful one. So, which one would you say was the biggest? Obama is the president and got there by lying. Hillary is still trying to buy it. I guess that makes Obama the best, maybe we could just call it a tie, with Bill running a close second. Three of the best Democrats that can be found across the world. No wonder the Democrats love them so much, with the help of the Antichrist Muslims and the Mystery Babylon Whore False Prophet, they have the country in the palm of their hand. Over twenty-trillion dollars in debt and promising their supporters more money if they will just reelect them again. The money printers have not run out of paper yet.

They have sworn to keep the guns out of the hands of the Christians that are causing so many murders over the world. Obama was telling us what we were thinking when he started running for president, said we were saying "He has a funny name" I've been looking at it eight years now and do not remember laughing at it one time. Said we were thinking "He just might be a Christion" I do not believe the thought every seriously crossed my mind. But I guess he was right about a lot of people, if they were not thinking it then, he got them to thinking it. He proved he is good at reading our minds, if he must plant the thoughts there himself. That is what he is so good at.

When I first heard his name that he chose for himself and was so proud of. It did not sound like a Christian name to me. I told them, when Carter was president, he was making a dirty word out of the name democracy, who wants it now? Obama and Hillary has finished it off nicely; it does not sound like a Christian name to me anymore either.

Like the talented man that started out with the Christian name, Cassusus Clay, from around Louisville, Kentucky. God had given him the talent and ability to become maybe the greatest fighter in the world.

He was obviously raised to be a Christian, with the evidence all over him his entire life. But was taken over when he was a teenager. He was used and abused, misled, and mistreated until he became so discouraged and started blaming God for all his misfortunes until he rebelled against God and accepted another god and a new name. I have written in this book how names denote character with God. He obviously just did not fit into that mold his name called for, and started on his way downhill. Lived a miserable life from that time on, until his death. I pray God will accept his suffering and chastisement as enough to pay his way into the glories of God. I did not see where he ever blasphemed the Spirit of God, of course it is not left up to me in any way. I know what I could see and I can pray for him. I believe it would be a safe wager to say the people that took advantage of him, spent his millions and pushed him back up for, as long, as he could go; will probably have to face more charges in judgment than Mohamed Ali will ever face. But he lost about all his chances to accumulate much fruit in the hereafter.

One can only accept for sure what one can see and read in the Word of God. But God says the things that are happening around us are there for our learning. I do not believe I want to accept Allah or Mohamad as my God. A blind man should see that, if he is told and can open his eyes.

Without any objection or complaint, one can state that O' Reilly is among the top intelligent people in our country and among the top news casters for fifteen years and counting as he says. But I wonder about his standing with God. I do not mean to try and judge him for he is around the top of people in my estimation. I have taken a liking to him as have millions of others. I do not feel like he will take any offence, I have used him before and mailed him a copy of the book. Got back a comment and sort of an apology from him through the TV set, with no names mentioned. He has very much of a Godly heart, I would give him a pass in a minute's time if it was up to me. But it is not. God says no man will be allowed to judge another man's soul.

That does not mean we are not supposed to be concerned about one another, as a matter of fact, it says quite the opposite. I know what denomination he believes and trust in. This is my main reason for concern, I know of a few million more quite like him, and all I must go on is what God's Word says. This should get anyone to where I am coming from, I hope.

These people do not acknowledge a born again experience into the life of Christ like the Bible teaches. The Bible teaches that without it we cannot be one in the Spirit of God with Christ, and the Holly Ghost. Now I hope you can see what I am talking about. I read in God's Word, God has told ever Christian to be apt to teach and be instantly ready in and out of season. But you will not find anywhere in the Bible that the God of this universe has used force or advocated his people to use force to get anybody to accept our serve him. A few times when someone was at the end of their rope, God's spirit came to them and offered them a deal or the consequences. Of course, the deal was always better, but with a price. This is the deal everybody has before them any time. God's people are asked to make the deal known to as many people as will hear, but never ordered to try to use pressure. Any religion that advocates force is not of Jesus Christ or the Spirit of the living God. It is a religion of Satan and you can count on it.

Our freedom of religion guarantees your freedom from anybody else's religion, and our government is ordered to not draw up a law to deny anybody freedom from their own religion because it is not allowed to enforce anybody's religious laws. But our heathen government has been making up all kinds of laws to regulate their own religion upon everybody else. Every one of them are unconstitutional and our Supreme Court should know it. But them and all our liberals are possessed by Satan's evil powers coming from the Mystery Babylon Whore Church there at Rome. Trying to do away with the Bible, and about to get it done. Read your Bible.

There has never been an election so clear as to the choice we have before us in the upcoming presidential election of two-thousand and sixteen, elections are. It is a chance for saving our country or sending it straight to hell, no variation. This, is why the devil-possessed Democrats, are and have opened up our borders to millions and millions of illegal Muslims for they are God haters sworn to kill the Christians and Jews from the earth and will vote 100% for the Democrat party and keep them in power over all the money printing machines. Any one that cannot see that is willingly deaf and blind, as I say, "They are Devil possessed."

I guess we should be praying for them ten kingdoms that are going to rise and eat the flesh off the Mystery Babylon Whore and burn her city off the earth. But, no need to pray for it, God has already said what he is going to do with it, but we have a chance to elect a God sent man like Donald Trump and if God's people will get behind him then much of this country can and will be spared through God's wrath which is for sure coming. And if not we will watch it go to hell. Which is what the liberals are working for. No marvel that they are wanting us to speak a foreign language. I kind of favor my country, myself.

As I have been writing, the Bible is written in a spiritual language. You can add all the words to your language you want to, just do not try to add them to God's language, he does not want them and does not need them. We should not be fooled, or try to fool anybody else by whose word we are speaking. We are either speaking God's Word from the Bible are we are speaking a carnal language which is just one's opinion. Opinions are, I say, one of the cheapest things on earth, you can pick up a pocket full from about anyone you meet and will not coast you a dime.

We are told to establish ever word of God from two are three witnesses are it is just one's opinion. God's Word properly preached and adhered too would eliminate all denominations but one. I know that is kind of shocking to someone that thinks his denomination, or anything else he holds up as his God, is going to save him, Jesus says he is wrong. Satan has conquered God's people and as Daniel said, division is the way he has taken them.

Denominations are the worst divider among them, when God's people are divided they are powerless. Satan is laughing at them before God every day. Read your Bible, what does God say about it? What else do we have, to study or lean on? God gave it to the English-speaking people and told them to preach it to the Greek and Hebrew and to ever creature in the world. I have never read where he ever said you can leave out the Greek and Hebrew, they already have their Bible. And I've never read where he told the Greek and Hebrew to preach theirs to us. Maybe you have, that is between you and your God. I'm just a little partial to mine, he is the Spirit, and the creator of everything, that has been created.

I have written some bit in all my books about how God created everything in this creation somewhat in twos. I do not believe I have dwelt too much on this, it is just too big and important and needed; to not be understood. God has told his people plainly, and in many ways, that his plan for us is to come together as one people, even into one body with God, Jesus, and the Holy Ghost. They are three but in the Spirit, they are one. The carnal just cannot receive and believe any such talk, as making any sense. Therefore, God has dismissed anything apart from God as being dead, as it takes the Spirit to give life, light, are anything else that is truth and real. Jesus said he came to divided. How can you divide anything without making two?

I would like to use the word, denomination, to try to explain a little farther. The word denomination is a carnal word, you will not find it in the Bible. God has not forbid us to use carnal words, but has forbid us to add them to his Word. His word (The Bible) does not need them and would be confusing to anyone in the Spirit if not explained as to how you are using them. It's easy, but dangerous to assume everybody is thinking the same way you are, and on the same track. If it is a Biblical word your church should know how it is used, for that is what you are doing speaking or talking to them; is to explain to the church where they can be understood. If your pastor cannot explain a word, from the Bible as God says for him to do, then he needs help.

Let me ask a few questions to get us on the same page together. Can you imagine an Assembly of God preacher going to a Baptist church and trying to teach them Assembly of God denominational doctrine? Are turn it just vice-versa you will have the same situation. Would you expect either one to bring them two into one in agreement? I don't think so.

They are both God's people and have taught their children to come together, all of them, with god's people and God's Spirit as one. When they cannot fit together, something is wrong. Anyway, that is what God's Word has taught. Which one of them are wrong? I have always thought that is what the church house was for, God's people to come together to be taught of the same Jesus Christ. Pray for one another and work out their differences and love and help one another. With the *Bible* as the guide (Which is Jesus Christ).

Not come together to convince everybody that nobody could be smart enough to bring two churches together and if he thought he could he would have to be a fool. God has said, *he* is not divided and there is not two of him. But they are right, no one person is going to bring the two churches together. But I believe the churches are the fools.

There is only one thing on earth that can bring two churches or two people together, that is the engrafted Word of God. And it will take the two churches agreeing to the same Word of God like it says to; read it and receive it. There is not two of them, how confused do you think God is? God says to establish every word that proceedeth from the mouth of God with two or three witnesses. Now that did not say every carnal word that comes out of man's mouth. Can you just imagine how much confusion that would bring on? Maybe you can see why God said he did not need one carnal word in his Word. He is not the author of confusion, but did author the Bible.

The promise from God, of a deliver, begins in Genesis. God told Moses he would raise up a prophet liken unto him. Said he would not be speaking his own words but would be speaking God's Words. And men would hear him, or their souls would be cast out from among my people. Everything in that Bible he has said to us, it is God's Word. It is Jesus Christ that was with God in the beginning, he was the Word before he was made flesh and dwelled among us. He has filled a lot of positions but has always been there and has always been the same even though he has not always appeared to us in the same form, it is still Jesus. There is only one Word of God. Tell that to a carnal mind. You will not get one to understand it.

Everything is revealed in the Word and the Word has revealed ever thing. God knows the future just as well as he knows the past, that is out of our comprehension but we have no reason to not believe him for the proof is all around us. God's every Word, is yea and Aman, if we just believe him there is no need for a lot of details or explanations. So, everything that is told about the same thing, in God's Word, is just more information, not a change or contradiction. And most things are told or mostly started early back in the Bible, and will be verified in at least two or three places, plus you will be given an example. Seems a sure way to verify and establish anything the Bible says. Why do people think it can be interpreted by each person as he pleases, and they could possibly be all right? Doesn't that sound a little foolish to anybody with a half sound mind, and one eye? We would have around seven billion versions in the world.

If anybody speaks to you something that cannot be established with two or three witnesses in the Word of God you can just take it for whatever it is worth, for it is not to be taken for Gospel before you check it out. To repeat it, you may be caught lying, so the Bible says.

God refers to it as tail bearing, busy bodies sowing discord, among his people and sees you as workers of iniquity, especially if it is none of your business.

I'd like to lay a little of the Bible story of Peter on us, some people have built a complete church history on him. No wonder they only believe parts of the Bible as one of them told me. They are only to believe the part their church tells them they can believe. That is somewhat like about every denomination I know much about. Even if they don't say so, it is what they like to believe. Join or die. That has greatly influenced every religion I know of in this world. I believe that is the church God describes in the seventeenth chapter of Revelations, seems to me every detail fits. It has ruled over kings, and greatly influenced every religion of every people on the earth and a bunch of our education of today. Even claiming to have possessed the keys to the kingdom from Peter, and don't believe in a spiritual baptism, which *is* the key. How did they do that? If they are so carnally spirited, can they not show us a key?

Peter was a very presumptive man and was quick to take the lead, and speak first. But very plainly was not always right, in other words was not completely infallible, as I have heard some people claim. Peter answered Jesus when he asks him who he thought Jesus was. He answered, "Thou art the Christ, the son of the living God." Jesus called him Peter, meaning pebble, like a piece of a rock. Saying, he would build his church upon that rock. Jesus, gave Peter a blessing of the keys to his kingdom, which he used at Pentecost. It was plain he was not speaking of the fleshly man Peter, and told us so. It would take a fleshly carnal mind turned over to a reprobate mind, uniquely told to us and described to us in the book to the Romans, to believe a lie like that.

Jesus was talking to the answer Peter gave and the spirit it was given to him from, and said so. He was given the keys to open the kingdom of God to the world, where and when the Spirit was to be given. First to the Jews at Pentecost, then to the Gentiles about nine years later, at the house of Cornelius. Does someone need to possess the keys and keep opening it up again and again? The complete scene was spiritually written. Jesus, only and always, talked the words of the Father, from the Father. They are Spirit and they are life, and meant somewhere between very little and nothing, to or of, the carnal side of man in any way, except being truth. They are still spirit and they are still life and the only thing we are given, that if engrafted, can save your soul. Jesus, or his words, are the tree of life. Written down in a spiritual language, by the Spirit, in the King James Authorized Version of the Bible.

Jesus started telling them how he was to go up to Jerusalem, be taken by the Gentiles, be beaten and crucified. Peter took hold of him rebuking him saying, he was not to let that happen.

Jesus called him Satan and told him to get behind him, for he was offensive and a hindrance to him and told him why. A while ago you were speaking the words of my Father, now you are speaking the words of men. How much intelligence does it take to understand that?

No wonder there are so many denominations that don't want their people to read or hear the Bible. They cannot read a spiritual language. It has carnally worked out so well the government has taken it up, or has it taken up the government? There is a threat on your liberty and life to say that the Bible is the truth. They will lay in wait to kill you. Just as Jesus said, they would put you to death and think they were doing God a favor. I am sure they are doing their god a favor, but not my God. All the false gods have taking up the slogan, join or die. More proof I'm not serving the same god they are. My God does not accept the name of Allah, Buda, Isis, Mohammad or any other of the multiple names man has come up with for him.

The story about Peter, during the crucifixion, he denied Christ three times. I figure more out of confusion than fear but it was plain he didn't have the goods at that time, to stand like he said he would. Jesus told him Satan desired to take him and sift him but he had prayed for him that his faith would stand. Peter's faith stood even when he didn't.

When Jesus delayed a little about reporting to them, Peter became a little impatient and decided he would just go back to fishing and led the others back with him. When they had fished all night, and had caught nothing, and coming back to shore Jesus was setting there cooking their breakfast. A very nice story there if you care to read it. Peter ended up getting a little thrashing there, and Jesus gave him some bit of instructions and told him what he was expected to do. Peter naturally wanted him to tell them all about John. Wrong again, Jesus said it is none of your business what happens between me and John. Peter was to just follow him and that was going to get his hands tied and him led to a place he did not want to go, speaking of the manner of his death.

Paul, writing the book of Galatians spoke of Peter being led back under the law. He withstood him to his face for he was wrong and was to be blamed. Peter was not preaching the gospel of faith and of the Spirit, they had been given from Jesus Christ. Jesus' gospel was not of the old law or carnal works, but was of the Spirit. If the gospel they were preaching was not Spiritual, then Jesus will not have done one thing for us. In other words, carnal works or letter of the law will profit you nothing. You cannot earn one piece of salvation by works, or your own holiness. We can lay up Spiritual rewards in heaven by our works for God, but nothing carnal will ever go there are will ever be needed there. And we must make ourselves Spiritual if we are going there to collect the Spiritual rewards. The things we work for and receive here on this earth, Jesus will not owe us a dime for it when we stand before him in judgment. We will have been paid for it here or we will be paid over there with Spiritual pay that we have sent up, if it glorifies God. Paul told Peter plainly, that this gospel that Jesus gave was of the Spirit only, and could be understood only by the Spirit. It is the truth, the whole truth, and nothing but the truth. Every word of it must be established by at least two or three witnesses before being preached as Gospel.

We have a big teaching that Peter was the one that set up the church in Rome and presided over it there. Another wrong, no evidence that I have ever saw, can give any proof or claim that Peter was ever in, or made it to Rome, certainly not in the Bible.

I've only received this revelation after seeking God for maybe a few years or so, troubled much as to why Peter had to receive such a horrible death just a few miles out of Rome, obviously never making it to Rome. Most of the world seems to know much about. He was on his way to Rome and was about to get there before Paul. God seems to have told me these things that I'm starting into, that may be more out of history than out of the Bible. The Bible is backing up the history well that I have been covering the past few pages.

After covering Peter's character and works and even his traits and habits a little, I seem to have been given this assumption. God was not going to be able to use Peter to go to Rome, of course he knew all along how the Babylonian beast that had settled at Rome was going to try to use him, and did. Jesus proved over and over that Peter could not have stood up to the pressure and the spirit that was at Rome, to take over the church that Jesus and his Apostles left at Jerusalem. Like Paul stood up to them. Peter could stand up to death like he said he could, and did, even to being crucified upside down and maybe skinned alive, like they said. But Peter would have obviously been led back like he had proven so many times. If he would have been allowed to go on to Rome, seems for some reason he just didn't have the wherewithal to complete the job at Rome. But he had used the keys that Jesus gave him to open the kingdom to the world, like Jesus said. Jesus found a man that could stand up to them at Rome.

We seem to have the clearest, complete, personal record of Paul as about any Christian in the Bible. I'm sure Jesus is very proud of him, an apostle called out of time, and seemed to have accomplished more labor than them all, as he put it. Paul seemed to make it plain that if he had not killed and persecuted Christians out of ignorance and had it on his conscience that he might not have been given the job to go to Rome himself. It took three hundred years for the beast riding whore church to get control. Then it had to join the church and claim the title of Christianity and used the church of Jesus Christ to lead the world into what is known as the dark ages.

After it took over the tittle of setting in God's seat, they killed and slaughtered in the world until the world was brought to maybe its lowest point in all its history, at least until that time. Just what could Christ do about it? He had turned it over to his church, and they would not come together in Christ name and were powerless. Many tens of millions had to be put to death before others would wake up and stand with them, then Jesus gave himself to them in the form of the King James Bible; written by the Holy Spirit.

Are we going through the same thing again? Jesus says we will, only because his people have dropped the ball, it was not Jesus Christ's fault. He became our sacrifice making us that would accept him; becoming one in the Spirit with him; by believing him. This makes him to become our scapegoat but only if we are willing to become one with him in agreement, he became our Bible. Becoming one with a denomination or a country that is not one with Christ, cannot save anyone. No people that has not had God as their Lord has ever risen to the height of running the world and prospered since Jesus has taken the government on his shoulders. Some will say, well, it will bring them closer to God and help that way. True, but it is the truth they taught and preached that brought them closer to God, not the denomination or the country. Give the glory to God like he said to. It was plain and sure the building of God's Word, the Bible, and it being preached and heard. Was what led the world out of the dark ages and built kingdoms like England and America. To dominate the whole world and lasted as long, as they let the Bible lead, teach and guide them. Now they are losing their dominion just like Daniel said they would, at the same ratio they are getting away from Christ.

We all should give the glory to God for the denomination and for what they did that was good, is the way that God says it is supposed to work. God gets all the glory is what he has said. The Whore was on the side with the Germans in both world wars but when we came out the biggest beast so decidedly they made great strides to appear to have been on our side all along. They swore they could and would ride us too, now they are doing it.

They said they would take us by vote was their words, and would start in by infiltrating our colleges and teaching our Bible and God out. How many Bibles do you count in our schools today? They said, when we get to turning out their doctors, lawyers, and their school teachers what will there be left? That has been declared in their manifesto close to maybe more than three hundred years ago, and that is exactly what they have done. I don't ask you to take my word for it, I'm a complete dummy, but if you have any interest in this great country of ours at all, you can check it out. But I know the most of you are just alike and do not have the time. It probably would not put one dime in your pocket or one beer in your hand so just sleep on. It is bound to be somebody else's fault anyway, so there goes all interest.

That seems to be the number one defense in anyone doing a wrong or making a mistake, or procrastinating, is to find someone to blame it on. If you don't want to believe that, just listen to any left headed politician, you can see it put-to-use, in every line. All lawyers are schooled in how to use it. Works well to, guess that is the reason that they use it so much. The Democrat party is built upon it and the others can only survive on it. It's all right to do these things to the world if you can get away with it, I guess. But don't bank on doing it with God. It's nice to always have someone to blame everything on, it is called a scapegoat. God is the one that showed us it would work. Then he became our scapegoat.

I've often thought the Democrats just allow enough Republicans to be elected to have around for a scapegoat. They almost run too many of them out of congress when Bush left. Didn't have enough of them left around when they pushed through Obama Care and didn't get a Republican to sign it. Blamed it on Romney anyway, saying he drew it up when he was governor of Massachusetts so it was his entire fault. Of course, the whole country bought it, hook line and sinker.

Must be nice to have the whole carnal establishment behind you, just show them the way you are leaning, throw out a few million or billions of tax payer's dollars in that direction and watch the dirty works and lies go to work. We have the best office holders and news reporters, and college professors, money can buy. I just have a hard time liking a hireling. Too many people got more money than me. I can vote for principals and can match a lot more people than I can with money. I do lose a lot of my votes, I believe if I get to vote for the man I wanted, I will not concede my vote as being lost. I tell them too, that I count my vote as two votes. One that my man got, and one that the other man didn't get. I can never understand somebody not voting, thinking he would just lose his vote. Sounds like fuzzy math to me, with gross ignorance, bordering on stupidity.

Seems that Confessing Christians should be smart enough to see that if they would come together, united like Jesus said, instead of tearing themselves apart and allowing every carnal thing under the sun to help divide them into little pieces like Satan wants. They could unite and become the biggest voting-block in this country, and about elect any president they chose to elect. Only the Democrats have figured that out. Reckon that is why God told us there is power in unity, and why the politicians hate the Christians so much. And certainly, do not want them to unite, and willing to kill, steal and lie to keep it from happening.

I don't blame them for if they were *true* Christians it would be the end of evil, politicians are evil. It is pure and simple why God gave us a Christian hater and killer for a president, God is trying to wake us up. It seems like most of us love the world so much they would rather play the part as zombies for the favors and free stuff it gives, than to live like God said. Obviously not interested in the favors God gives. They are not to the greedy flesh. God is all a Spirit, if we are not willing to be born into the Spirit, we will not fit into his spiritual kingdom.

The power that God has promised us is in unity. If Satan can keep us divided, we have no power at all and will be laughed at by Satan before God every day. People had better wake up; Jesus Christ is in one Spiritual body and comes no other way. If we are walking in his Spirit, we are in his body. Equal to everybody else that is in his body.

The only requirement I see much about that God has given us for voting for, is to put them to rule over you that rule in the fear of God. You would think someone knowing God could listen to any two-people campaigning and know which one gives God more credit for good, than blame for the bad, than the other one. Someone that can't, would raise a question in my mind who he was voting for, God or himself? In any election, you only have one vote for the man you think is best.

Of course, that is talking legally. I am aware that are voting system is so full of fraud it cannot hold a sack of corn shucks. But will about promise you that the lying Est crooked Est side of about any election is the side the most of the so-called Christians are voting on. So why should we complain?

Christians are more divided than the heathen that will tell you he is voting for himself and could not care less about God. At least the heathen is not being a hypocrite or a liar. Someone claiming to be working for God and voting for self is a little bit or completely both.

The first book I wrote was titled "Killing-Self" this is what I was writing about in it. God has no use or need for self in any situation I know of, and certainly not in voting against God's principles in any election. It had better be for God in everything, if he wants to be called from heaven, a *Christian*. God told me to put his principles in front of everything; see everything through his laws and principles.

A house divided cannot stand. Man, is going to kill and destroy himself unto a very low point. I'm beginning to wonder how low Christians are going to volunteer to allow themselves to be beaten down, mostly by one another, and act like they are enjoying it.

I wrote where God told me that it was not him that was giving that Antichrist power over the saints and to put them to death. It was his church; and by us being divided is a sure way to get it done. We cannot save ourselves divided, not to mention be a light to the world; and save someone else. That would be out of the question.

The Bible teaches very plain this would happen, and there would be a falling away before Jesus comes back. I'm starting to think the falling away was a vast understatement on God's part. It looks more like a train wreck to me, but he did say a *great* falling away; and the world would take off after the Antichrist in the last days. So, I guess he did have it covered. Them that do not read or hear the Bible will not be prepared; will not be expecting him and will be surprised.

Most of the things Jesus named are starting taking place now. Jesus said they would be saying that he has delayed his coming. I have not heard that being preached yet. I have been looking for it to show up, for I believe Jesus meant some would be preaching it. And I believe it will be just before his return so it is getting about time to hear it. They can add it to the many other lies and false doctrines that they are so strongly pushing down our kids throats with no resistance from anybody I see. With over half of the world saying if you disagree with us you will be killed, and the number is growing. That is the spreading of Mystery Babylon told about in the book of Revelations, for end times.

They are already being gathering up, eating the flesh off the Mystery Babylon Whore, by the Antichrist and Lucifer spirits that are plaining to kill Christ at Armageddon. It is being called the war on Christianity that is going on in the world today, led by the Antichrist spirits of the ten kingdoms. Why do so many people choose to believe these, man-made gods that exist for nothing but to kill, steal, and destroy, instead of believing Jesus Christ? He is the only one that can promise life. Where can a man-made god get life for you from? It is man that hates the Bible, not the spirits; they are scared to death of it. Man, does not have that much sense. He tries to fight and destroy it for the Devil that he must spend an eternity in hell with. Not very smart, for you will not receive any profit or gain in kissing up to the Devil, he has already lost. Jesus asks what have you gained if you gain the world and lose your soul. We are going to spend eternity with our choice.

Speaking of being smart, our country is being run by doctors, lawyers, judges, politicians, and queers that do not have enough common sense to look at a baby and tell if it is a male or a female. One must wait until it is-able-to talk and ask it how it feels. I know that is unbelievable, but it is true. Just listen to what they are telling you and our kids, unless they have got you as fooled as they are. Apparently, a many voter has become just that stupid while teaching our kids in every school, it is the normal and they better not disagree with them. 0ur college kids have not been told any different, but the same things. Parents are that dumb, are else scared to death, or just don't give a dam, I believe it must be a combination of the three.

Every which way, the results are the same, and doesn't show much hope for improvement to anyone who has any common sense. It gets depressing just to look across this country at the level of intelligence of our people. And no one is doing anything about it. God is the giver of knowledge. How can one tell a person anything when he is convinced he already knows it all? Donald Trump must find someone to join him that is willing to become smarter, in-order-to make this country great again. He sure has my prayers. I think I will try to write a chapter on finding an individual to maybe help him a little.

Living is a learning process, if you are not dead you should be learning. A person's mind is constantly allowing thoughts to pass through his mind in and out. If they can keep passing out while none are coming in, he will eventually end up with a blank mind. Some might call that dead, while some cannot do that kind of math. Therefore,

Jesus said he came to bring us life, and more abundantly, he is the giver of knowledge.

Anything with life must have food, if you cut off its food it will die. Jesus is our food.

Satan and his slaves can only give lies and perversion, for the purpose to kill, steal, and to destroy. Satan is the father of all lies; seems he has children everywhere, and they are his slaves. If you are a liar no need to think you have God for a father, he does not claim you. He will not feed you food that will kill you.

CHAPTER 10

GOD, HAS A JOB FOR YOU

The Bible teaches, everybody has a calling and a place, each one consists of many callings and many places. Everything has-to be directed by the Spirit of God, to fit into his plan and the fellowship of his son. That volunteered to be born into a fleshly body like yours and mine. He took it back to the father as a sacrifice for all mankind to have a chance to become something permanent in God's plan.

They both sent back the Holy Spirit that could give us all a new birth into the Spirit, becoming as one with him and the Father. He left the keys with Peter. He gave his body to become our sacrifice that he could become the scapegoat for us. All we had to do was to become a willing, useful, servants, in the kingdom of God, with his Spirit in us as a guide and helpmate. All of this is a spiritual thing, apart from the carnal.

Jesus died for our sins, and sin cannot separate anybody from Christ; but when one gets it accepted into his heart and becomes a part of him, that person will become separated from God if he does not repent and put it away.

Scapegoat is like any other word; it can be used in two directions. Satan is a copier and the bottom and back side of God. He can use the word in his direction with anything he can get control of. We should just never let him have control of anything about our flesh. Our flesh is on his side; apart from God, carnal.

Jesus, the Spirit and the Father are one. That is where we completely lose the carnal flesh. We are born into their Spirit to become a new creature. The flesh cannot have that spirit; it becomes just a house to contain the new creature in, for its time on earth.

Now try to pick this up; we've had a spirit in us as long, as we have had life. It was given to us by God when we were born into the flesh. Handed down to us through the flesh, by the flesh, belonging to us, the one it was born to. Apart from God as all flesh is. It was subject to the flesh that we were in. If we want to move into the Spirit of God and become one with God and his Son by their Spirit. The flesh doesn't have one thing to do with it, except die out, for it is always at war with the Spirit; it is on Satan's side. We either choose Jesus for life, or Satan for death.

In the spirit, there is neither male or female. Maybe our country is trying to deny the flesh and claim they are spiritual, not knowing which sex they are. That would be nice but that requires us to know what spirit we are of and live like we are in the Spirit and I don't believe I can see very many that meets that requirement among them that has forsaken their God given habitat. It doesn't even need to put on an act for their neighbor, to convince him. Just start living like it, your neighbor will notice. The flesh does not change, maybe your countenance, but that is not a requirement it just happens. We die out to the flesh; it is completely a spiritual action. The closest thing to being your spirit in your body I know of, is your mind. You cannot see your mind; neither can you see your spirit. But evidence of both sticks out of your whole body everywhere. That should tell you a bunch.

The Bible teaches much about your mind all threw it. We are told the glorious light of the gospel, shines through our minds to our heart that you can be saved. But it can be blocked in your mind by Satan, if you allow him to. So why can we not call this completely a mind thing? Your mind controls the rest of your body, including your spirit and heart. When it doesn't, Jesus calls that blind.

Being baptized into the death and body of the Lord Jesus Christ is completely a Spiritual thing. I do not see where water has one thing to do with it, any more than a testimony, and an outward commitment. It is all in your mind. Water cannot wash your mind, but God says his Spirit can. God teaches that he can use a made-up mind, but a double minded person need to not expect to receive anything of the Lord. A double minded man is unstable in all his ways; playing to both spiritual and carnal sides. So, if you want to move into a new creature, called the Spirit of God, then take on a completely made up mind and a new boss, learn his ways, his laws, (Laws of Christ, not old testament laws even though they are perfect) and his principles. Jesus is a Spirit and a complete replacement for anything carnal and connecting us to God. Take on his very mind; maybe most important of all learn his voice. That may take some time, but you will have the rest of your life here on earth to learn. It will take all of it and God will still have a few surprises for you. One thing I learned shortly after I accepted Christ. I had received a complete new set of values. Took a little getting used to, but I learned very quickly to love them.

If it is not an enjoyable ride, then you can be sure you have not put down your flesh out of the way far enough. It is the only enemy that can touch you. If you let it, it can destroy you any day of the week. It is always trying to take back control, and get in the driver's seat.

See if you can follow this, your mind is to control your spirit, to align it with the Spirit of God which is to control everything in and about your body. Keep a few facts in your mind; the Spirit of God; the Word of God; Jesus Christ; God the Father; are four Spirits with four functions, but like the Father, Son, and Holy Ghost are three, yet they are one. These are four yet they are one. You can only receive that by faith, which is nothing but believing God.

Therefore, God stresses faith so much, without it you can never please God. Your flesh cannot please God for it cannot believe God. Therefore, it can have no faith is why it must die, it is always waring with the spirit. Your mind and your spirit must always remain under subjection to the mentioned four. These four are definitely-four but you can never separate them they are one in agreement, principle, purpose, they are just one, you just have-to believe it. Only the spirits are like this but they are all that way to some degree. Jesus can cover the whole world, enough to be in every person on the globe I suppose, but isn't. The Antichrist obviously can occupy maybe a few million bodies or more. The False Prophet can occupy every pope in the Mystery Babylon Church riding the beast there at Rome, him and the Antichrist. Do not ask me to explain these things about spirits they just are not held to the same abilities as people. One third of them rebelled and caused a war in heaven.

Lucifer was their leader and was defeated and threw out of heaven. It seems that all of us are given an allotted time I have no idea of how it is measured out.

The war is not over yet for the demons talked to Jesus of their allotted time. I believe it is also called a cup of inequity, everybody seems to be carrying one, and is allotted time to get it filled. John wrote of the last battle that is yet to come, and the writers wrote of big angels and angels of different rank and assignments, and strength and favor with God.

God has plenty of room in his kingdom. The door is still wide open. He will not mix with carnal only through Jesus; he became the mediator between us and God. Or no flesh or anything about it could be saved, so don't grieve him. No false god can acknowledge him. They tend to choke on just his name, for all Satan's spirits know who Christ is, maybe the person doesn't know him but his spirit does, and cannot hide his hatred, love nor fear of him. They cannot hide from Jesus that is in you. If they rise just against you, better be careful. Try to get them into a confutation with the Spirit of Jesus Christ; that is the Word you know. You need all of it you can get for it can cast him from a vessel into outer darkness, but you can't. Satan knows it very well, and if you do not have enough of the Spirit of God to defeat him, he usually knows that too, and willing to take a chance on it, if he can take control or not. That is called being tested.

We are in a battle whether we know it or not, it is with our flesh. If we are not in a battle with our flesh, then you must not have much of the Spirit of God in you. Or maybe your flesh is dead as it ought to be. Most churches rather call on none believers to settle their problems in church than to trust in the Spirit they have in the church to handle it. In most cases, I've witnessed, that was probably a smart move, but Paul said, dare you to take a brother to law, before the unbelievers, to settle a dispute *in the church.* If you do not have someone in charge among you smart enough to settle a problem, just ask the smallest one among you. He can tell you the difference in right and wrong, just and unjust. It is almost always over authority and who is going to set in God's seat. The Word of God is the only one that is qualified to set there. A pastor cannot fill that chair; it takes the Word to help him.

The one is in charged is supposed to be the one that is to be preaching, teaching, and explaining it to the church. But most of them are too busy preaching what they have been told and their opinion and not doing their job or the problem would not have raised that high in the first place. The Word of God (Bible) is any Christian's only weapon. If we don't know it, we are defenseless. Without an offensive weapon, we just have-to put on the rest of the armor of God and let them beat on us. That is when it is mighty handy to have a good man of God close by that does know something about the Word of God and is not afraid of a little spiritual battle, and willing to help.

In this battle, as in any battle, there are many positions and plenty of room to work. Anybody being led by the Spirit of God, walking in his will, will never be rubbing shoulders with someone else that is walking the same. If they are bumping together one of them is walking a little off course, probably both are a little off. That causes two in the same ranks to start killing on one another. Much of that would weaken any army.

That don't mean the both of you bend a little to fit together. It means both of you get into the Word and get straight and you can walk a hundred miles and still be walking together and never rubbing each other, amazing! You should try it. There is a multiple of power in unity. Everybody is pulling in the same direction you will just not be easily defeated; God has promised us that. That church will have power. Satan can see it and will tremble in his boots.

You should know yourself, know what you are called to do, know what you can do, what you are attempting to do, know if you should try to do it or not. God told us to be quite to mind our own business. We should know what our business is. This is where knowing the Spirit is a must. A communication with God is vital. If you don't have one, you better have a close leader in the church that does. One you can trust; good to have a church full you can trust. Watch out for jealousy and bitterness, in yourself and them. They are killers.

Most of us know better than to try picking up a three-hundred-pound rock by ourselves, but there is some that just wants to keep on trying. Sooner or later he is bound to hurt himself if he tries too hard. God told us to prepare and allow help, and use wisdom. Anyone that is not in unity would be riding the rock instead of lifting. Or maybe setting on the rock, trying to lift it. He will have-to be carried. We need to know how many we can carry. It is hard to beat patience and common sense in any situation. No need to ever be varying in truth for truth doesn't vary.

Carnal has just about thrown them both out of everything, and what it hasn't, it is still trying. Satan is not giving up on anything until he gets threw alive into the lake of fire at the end of the battle of Armageddon, where the Antichrist beast and the False Prophet already are. God is not going to need him anymore, for he will not have anybody left who needs tested. The Dragon will be thrown into the lake of fire, with the Antichrist, and the False Prophet, in that order. Them with Christ have all been proven with their names written in the Lambs book of life. Don't fail when you are tested, overcoming chastising, always brings a growth and peace to the overcomer. But one must overcome, or he will be thrown into the lake of fire.

God has endless callings and places for all the people who wish to be converted from the carnal into the Spiritual. From serving the world, which is material, flesh, carnal, and anything we can see and handle. And get into serving God which is a Spirit and of a different world which we can see and handle only with our minds, and that by faith. The Spirit comes to us in the form of light and life, how heavy is that? How much can you hold in your hand? How long can you hold it in a sack? Yet light may be the most powerful thing man has encountered. Ever try tackling a lazars beam? X-rays work by controlled light, so does almost everything else. Including a tree growing in the woods.

When an angel of God shows up in the Bible, it is about always with, and as a great light.

The carnal callings, or maybe habitats, consist of males, females, fathers, mothers, husbands, wives, and lots of children of all ages. Each calling is a position; in each position has many jobs, some of them we cannot change. Males will stay males, females will stay females regardless of the body parts they change, it will remain very difficult to fill any positions and assignments within any other calling and impossible to fill them all.

But some of us try but will probably fail, and we must allow some kind-of-place for freaks. I'm sure God will take care of that, he might use you right there. Children will remain children until they grow into adulthood. God knows the how, why, and everything else of anything. But you can be sure if God made a person a male he intended him to operate in that capacity and calls it his given habitat, estate, calling, and position. He will be judged from the Word of God on how he performs his duty within his calling. I am sure one can count on it, despite all the carnal reasoning one can come up with.

As I have said all along, God didn't make man to give God advice on anything. I'm sure he gets quite a bit of that, and I'm sure he does not need it. He didn't make man for complaining either, got a problem, tell God, he will hear but he doesn't like griping or complaining. Do not every argue with him, he is there to help you.

There are lots of jobs and duties for each calling, all to be under, unto, and for, a living God that is over everything. We should be happy that he is a fair, just, and all righteous God, perfect in every way. We are not forced to be under another spirit for there is not another spirit apart from God that can be a righteous spirit. But being willingly ignorant we choose another spirit and blame a righteous God for all the misery it brings. It is here for no other purpose but to kill, steal and destroy. When we choose to be a slave to it we want to be just like it for we are led away from God only by our lust and believing a lie. I'm sure it's hard for God to understand us, we will not believe him when he has never lied to us, and choose to believe a spirit that has told nothing to us but lies. He swore his Spirit would not always strive with man, and I'm sure he meant it.

Man, is called to be the head and father to his entire house and everything in it. With responsibility to God of course, for God is the head of everything. If a man's house consists of another man he is to be under the man of the house or get out and start his own house. If he stays he is to help the head of the house and they should both put God first. Put their trust in the real God, not their god. This principle is applied to anything. Therefore, there is no other God, there is no other Word of God. There is no other way you can bring two things into one but only in spirit, and truth. Then it must be the same spirit if they are to be one. If they are in two different spirits, there are two of them instead of one. Seems to me a carnal mind should be able to see that, except a carnal mind cannot see a spirit. He just must believe. Like we have said it is a mind thing.

Can you just visualize a country or nation that was built with God being the head and all men coming together to please him? All they would have to do is speak and the rest of the world would roll over. God's plan is to come together, one with him, so they would have to be in unity for the world to roll over. Be humble and he can supply every need, but if they can't agree as one then he could not please two people apart from him. Just as sure as one was praying for a rain the other would be over at his place unknowingly praying for a sunny day so he could get the rest of his hay in. Now how is God going to please them both?

Of course, they would think that God should rain on one place and send sunshine on the other, but what about their close neighbors? Would they all be happy? God says for them to come into agreement and work together with him and he will work out all your needs. Who do you think could get several hundred denominations together? If you know one, I bet you could get him a good high paying job working with the Lord. My point is, there is a reason for God telling us we need to work with him. He is the best boss I've ever worked for and I could come up with a list of good bosses.

Any other spirit's plan is to divide and conquer; steal us from God to make slaves out of us for his pleasure, or kill us. Does that remind you of any carnal religions that you know of? Even sounds like a modern politician to me especially the ones we have running things for us now. I didn't vote for very many of them for sure. I told as many as I could what these antichrist politicians were doing but said if they could stand it so could I. And so far, I have done very well, but sorry for them. God is the one that provides for me and he can do that even when the Muslims get their flag up over our white house. It is looking like we don't have a great deal of time to wait to see it. I can hear the question you want to ask, "Do you think that is really going to happen?" Let me answer that with my own question. Who do you think is going to stop them? As Jesus said once, you answer my question, and I'll answer yours. Their flag has gotten more respect and authority from our government and federal judges than ours has. Whose flag got authorization and guaranteed protection by our Supreme Court, to be burned in public? It was not the Muslim's flag.

The Bible says blessed is the nation whose God is the Lord. Is the Lord setting in the top seat in this country now? The obvious answer is no, so we are obviously not being blessed. If we don't change, we are not going to be.

The women were created to be a helpmate for their man, to help their man in all his Godly duties. Raise the children in the fear and admonition of the Lord, keepers at home, teach the young women to grow up to do the same, always acknowledging the man as their head even between them and God. If any wife cannot agree to that she is free to go and the husband is no longer tied to her. I do not believe our country will be one bit worse off if they leave. They are free to remarry but only in the lord, the same instructions are what the Bible teaches, should be good and plain enough for all of us. God has called us to peace.

The children are called to honor their parents and fully obey them in the Lord. The first commandment from the Lord with a promise from the Lord tacked to it, that they might have a long life here on the earth. Parents are told, under the law, if a child cannot be controlled, to take him before the congregation and let them stone him to death. I know we are no more under the old law, which was perfect, nothing wrong with it and it will never be changed until all be fulfilled. Jesus did not do away with it but fulfilled his part in it and replaced the old priesthood. Took the government on his shoulders and we are now under the laws of Christ. Them that will not receive Christ are under the world's laws and will be judged as such.

Them that have excepted Christ are spiritual and have a new covenant which is with the Kingdom of God. It is completely spiritual, and it had not been given to men until after the crucifixion. It is called the Holy Ghost sent back and given to men through being baptized into the Spirit of Jesus Christ's death and resurrection; by and into the Spirit of God. This is the sum of the complete New Testament that probably a million sermons could, and may have already been, preached on, and still have plenty left to be preached. Therefore, God said over and over that each of us should study the scriptures; they are God talking to us and explaining.

Jesus did away with the old covenant, fulfilled the old law, paid the price for our redemption, and became everything for us. Made us complete in him, but we must be in him for anything. Without him we will pass on, having nothing. There was no law that could be given to completely forgive and free us from our sins or give us eternal life but Jesus the only begotten son of God did. Hopefully, let me use some of my own words to tell this story just for, maybe, a little better understanding.

Jesus is the son of God, or a part of God. Maybe just a small piece of God that volunteered to empty himself of his glory; and become a seed of Abraham planted in flesh. Born of flesh and grown into a body of flesh just like you and me. Becoming a human kinsman to us and being limited to a body of flesh. Tempted in every way just like every one of us. Carnal, or apart from God; just like us, yet without sin. He is the only fleshly man that has accomplished that. Jesus learned from his sufferings as he grew. He was given the Spirit from the father as is available to each of us today, thanks to Jesus. Because he did not let us down. Not even at the torturing and the crucifixion on the cross and his own Father allowing him to die. He did not have to go through with it, he could have changed his mind at any point. But he didn't, for his love for us and the glory that he was to receive when it was finished.

Sounds like the same deal given to us except we can accept his death, believe and be baptized into it, which is a spiritual thing. He died for us so we could live for him. And God will receive us as his children, brother to his begotten son Jesus. We will not have to give our life as a dead sacrifice, but a living. We can use Jesus' sacrifice and live forever more. You must believe, love, accept, and trust him. It must be genuine love for truth and righteousness; for you can never fake or fool him.

It would be a miserable eternity for both of you, if you do not love truth and righteousness, for he is nothing else. Sounds like a small price to pay for eternal life with him, instead of an eternity in hell. Where everything that does not accept, him is going, the only alternative. "Praise God for Jesus Christ"

Have you read in Isaiah where the Spirit said in the last days, the world will be turned around backwards? Calling good evil and evil will be called good. I believe the word backslidden is one-word God has used to name that condition; the word fool or fooled is some more. Some denominations I know will not accept there is such a word in the Bible as the word backslide. They should read the Bible; they might be shocked just a little. They can probably find a few more things in there they were not aware of. They will never learn them all in one lifetime, but by studying and the help of the Spirit of God we can learn enough. This is a promise of God.

CHAPTER 11

GOD HAS LAID HIS ARM BARE TO US

The word duped is not found in the Bible, so it is a carnal word. I will not try to add it to God's Word, but I looked it up in Webster's dictionary. I believe it may be the best word to describe the condition to a carnal person that does not understand a spiritual language. They have been duped; fooled and turned around. They are not going toward heaven, but the opposite direction. The world is heading in that direction. God has said for us not to follow the multitude; I can see why.

Jesus is the Word, and no man can say that he is not and not be a liar. No man is qualified to argue with him on any part of it. Only a fool would think he could. I do not intend to point out a problem, and not have the answer. The Word of God does not do that anywhere in it. If one will just humble himself, and hear it with an open ear and a little common sense, it has the explanations for everything it has said. In God's language is where God has laid his arm bare.

I have written that God is the author and giver of common sense; and how our colleges have been laboring around the clock to stomp out any evidence of common sense, they hate it. It reveals truth and lies the same and condemns anybody to hell that does not love truth.

Anything that filters down through our colleges and hits the ground, spreads out across the country and across the earth, like a huge tree dropping its leaves and fruit. A very dangerous place for the world, to be feeding from. For it is fatal to the Word of God. Colleges have become brain washing institutions for our youth. With their globalization ideas, they claim they are helping other countries. But have only torn our country down to the bottom of the heap. Only thing that will help and feed other countries is Jesus Christ. We cannot hold to him for our self, so it is sure we cannot hold to him for other countries. He is that Bible that Satan and the Mystery Babylon Whore Church is so determined to destroy out of our schools and off the earth. We will not be able to hold up one country if we cannot hold ourselves up. And we cannot do anything without Jesus. As Benjamin Franklin referred to him, as the builder of nations.

The politicians plan of community organization and transformation that sounds so good to a blooming idiot with no common sense, is not even starting to work out well. Our Democrats, busy telling us constantly how much better off we are getting, if their name was Pinocchio their nose would be so long they could not carry it. They would look peculiar, grown to a nose that they could not carry. If you don't get that, it means they are liars. If each of their lies were a snowflake, we would never be able to dig ourselves out.

They have been educated by the Mystery Babylon Whore that Jesus showed John in the wilderness and explained to him what it was, in the book of Revelations. She is a good set-up plan to not build anything up, but to tear this country down below the other countries. No excuse for us not knowing what is happening, we have been warned with an explanation. But of course, why would a smart educated man need to read such a low form written book, thousands of years old? It is God's arm, is one good reason. But we think we have become so smart in our amount of time, we do not need God. Turn that around and you will have it more correct. I can see why our educated college professors hate common sense so bad. They have been educated by the Mystery Babylon Whore Church that has been commissioned by Satan himself to rule the entire world over Jesus Christ and to kill on him forever. Jesus is common sense, and condemns Satan to hell on every corner. He gave the earth to us but we lost it to the father of lies; that has killed hundreds of millions of Jesus' saints and prophets.

I have never read where Jesus ever killed a spirit, but I have never read where a spirit ever stood up face to face with Jesus for battle, until the last few chapters in the book of Revelations. Appears to be maybe one of the shortest and bloodiest battles on record. I hope to be riding with Jesus.

Jesus became one of us to redeem us back, but we must be changed into his Spirit to hang onto anything about him. How so few people can see that, and not want it; or want it and not see it, I do not know. I guess we just love our chosen father too much to let go of the world's lies. We need to change our father; Satan enslaves all his children one way are the other. They become slaves to him. Try telling an alcoholic to quit drinking, or a dope addict to give up his dope habit even when he knows he is dying from it. You can probably learn a little something there, if you have a little common sense; humble yourself a little and use it.

Fathers are smarter than their children. I reckon they just give up trying to teach them anything. It being so much easier to let someone else do it. Satan is more than ready, with plenty of help. God says that is neglecting one's duty and God given responsibility, called procrastination. He has warned us of all these things I been writing about, in the Word of God. Even about the False Prophet spirit set up in Rome that has very subtly taken over our country while we are sleeping. Like Satan told us and God, he would do. But God has said, I have a few that will stand. Read the book of Job; meet one of them.

It is no wonder why God has told us so many times to awake out of sleep, hear, and prepare for battle. He has said, just a little folding of the hands, just a little sleep and poverty will come upon you. Made it plain he was speaking both physical and spiritual, as does most of the rest of the Bible. I do not know one word in the Declaration of Independence or the Constitution that says any citizen should worship any certain god or religion in this world. They have not been put *over* the Bible, and was not meant to be put over the Bible in any way. But it is plain they were both written to in no way, dishonor the God of our creation; the one God of Israel; or this one nation under God. It gives us our rights, liberties and freedom to seek our own happiness, if it did not hinder the next man's freedom living under the same laws and freedoms that you have.

But judgment of political laws which are contrary to God's laws and any common sense, cannot be enforced without force and oppression against our constitution. God's laws are based on truth, while political laws are based on a political party. I told them years ago, when they first started teaching political correctness, that as far as I was concerned, they could put it into their ears. If they were not contrary to God's laws they would not need laws to live at peace with one another. I was not one bit interested in them. God did not commission them to set in God's seat, but they are sure trying.

Hillary, with her mentor, Saul Lewinsky, that wrote the infamous book on how to radicalize a kingdom, giving Lucifer the credit, by basing all his knowledge on him; dedicating his book to Lucifer. Hillary has used it for a guide since before she got out of college until today, and has perfected it beautifully. She has duped a country with the world well in her fantasy view. She is an amazing woman, but can give a person with common sense, nightmares.

Now they have gotten our country turned upside down, but I reckon the women, queers, dope heads, gangsters, rioters and all other God haters are happy. They make up Obama, Hillary and Bill's standing army; and are very dangerous. Despising any authority that does not come from them. It gives the women freedom from their men, that God gave them to, but it did not give them freedom from God. It gives the sexes freedom from themselves, but not freedom from God. It gives the children freedom from their parents, but not freedom from God. It gives the illegal aliens and gangsters freedom from our laws, but gives nobody freedom from God's laws. So, some blooming idiots trying to help the Democrats out, formed an organization to get us, a <u>freedom from religion,</u> liberal law passed. To them, Jesus is the only religious thing on earth. Everybody can have their own god; just do not call him Jesus, or mention the Bible. Do you reckon God will be scared to violate a Democrat's freedom from Jesus law? I would not bank real heavy on it. But there is a lot of people that are just that stupid?

Maybe I should not complain, for we cannot offend them for sure. Our Democrat attorney general has warned us not to, and saying to disagree with them could be offensive to them, and she will prosecute. They may can take freedom away from the Christian white man but I don't believe they will ever fill God's seat. They have no idea that God, not the Christian white man, is running this world. I'd hate to be the one that would have to wake them up, could get your head cut off. God is not afraid of them I'm sure. Therefore, the Democrats and other duping politicians are so determined to eliminate all white men holding onto a God and gun. I am not threatening anybody, just naming a fact, I have not forgot how to use my gun; and strongly resent the thought of having my head cut off while my hands are tied. Especially when I see people all around me that would enjoy doing it.

Our Supreme Court has ruled no less than two times, this is a Christian nation (in 1892 and in 1932). It has never been challenged in court and remains to this day as the official U S Supreme Court opinion. I guess the God haters just forgot. Since the Obama administration, we have had a rash of attacks on Christians and Jesus himself; while telling, us they are enforcing the constitution, while Trump is not smart enough to. My Bible says, them that are accusing someone else are guilty of the same. I wonder why God is so smart and is always right.

I keep asking where are the Christians at that Christ has said would stand up for him? They must be dead, I do not believe they could sleep through all of what is going on and not know about it. I have decided they do not exist or have turned into Obama and Hillary worshipers. I would suggest to you that is why so many of the males are switching to females. And do not know the difference in what they are. You just mention one of their names if you want to get a rail out of one of them. Anybody that is grown and can look down at his body and not see and know if he is a male or female and not know that he needs help, let me interrupt here and tell him, "He needs help."

I have written in other places about radicalized. The word is not mentioned in the Bible meaning it is a carnal word. As I've said, the Bible has got it covered, the best I could come up with is *Devil-possessed.* I could find no real difference in the two words. Our left headed politicians have been taken over by the Devil himself. I have had no less than three people tell me plainly "They were born a Democrat, raised a Democrat all their life, and they will die a Democrat." I do not doubt their word and they are well within their rights, but don't try to tell me that person is not possessed with something. She needs help. Our parents, schools and churches are not the place to get it. They need help to. They are the ones that taught her such *nonsense.* How could someone swear such an oath and not be possessed with something? It is certainly not the Spirit of God like God's children are told to be possessed by. Of course, this one was one of them that has read her Bible clear through and reads in it every day. I know she does for I ask her and she told me she did. I'll not comment any farther about that one. But, I believe them kind will lie about other things too. My whole book is about this situation.

You would be amazed to know all I learn, while writing these books. The definition of the word *nonsense* that I used a few lines ago, is one with no common sense, coming from God's dictionary.

It is my opinion that top Democrat politicians are some of the most lying, possessed, hypocritical people on earth. If you study your Bible you can see it plain. They have a vast number of radicalized organizations trying to radicalize our nation, financed and pushed by such atheist as the Lame Stream Media, millionaires like Soros and Moore, college professors, Hollywood, the list is endless. People that my Bible sends to hell. Therefore, they hate it much; and have declared war on it; and anybody that will speak the Word in public. You going to tell me that you are a Christian and cannot see this? No marvel that Jesus said you were *blind*. I feel like adding a bunch more words to it that they are, but will try to reframe myself, unless asked.

They could cut my head off, burn my Bible; it would not keep it from sending them to hell. Just to not love truth is enough to do that. Truth is, common sense being revealed. It is the deadly enemy of all evil. It will destroy evil on contact. A great hate exists between the two, they cannot exist together without a battle going on. Each person can get on the side of his choice and fight as hard as he pleases. My books are written on this very subject. Does not God say we are in a battle and waring every day?

Our legal system from the top to the bottom has been transformed by the Mystery Babylon Whore and her Antichrist False Prophets. Until truth has been threw under the bus for political correctness that claims it is the government's own Bible and God. And sets in the seat of Christ, calling itself the vicar of Christ and does not recognize the baptism of the Spirit of God. Christ will not recognize them on judgment and has said so very loud. At the judgment, Jesus, will see two kinds of people, them with his Spirit and them that do not have it. That is a part of the Bible their church does not believe, ask one of them. Their pastor has told them not to answer you. Don't be surprised at the answer you get. How much would you figure a salvation that you could not talk about would be worth?

With billions of people, there will be no time for debate; he will have his rewards in his hand for each person when he shows up. There may be time but God has never put up with any arguing from flesh. His word has been there for debate from the time of our birth. If nobody has explained it to you, blame your parents, they were the ones responsible for starting you off right or wrong; not the government. And each Christian has some responsibility to carry it on threw, with the Word of God. He promised to appear unto each person at least one time. I am sure he has or will, but he is a Spirit and flesh will not recognize him if it is not interested.

Our homes and schools have thrown out the word responsibility some years ago, along with a lot of other Godly words. This country is suffering from that act unto almost annihilation. I don't believe this generation has hardly heard of it. Responsibility starts in the home and family and should be tended and grown, but we do not have homes and families as God has recognized, anymore. We gave that to the government. What we didn't give them, they took.

One mistake we have made is, we have allowed Satan's people to preach our gospel to us, we are not responsible to Satan's people, just to God's, and that being toward Godliness. Therefore, I say we need to know the difference between the spiritual and the carnal.

Our government has replaced all responsibility with tic knowledge. I remember when the TV first came out; they said they would be the best teaching tool every made; the day was coming when we could just set our children down in front of one and teach them at home and not have to send them off to school. How did that work out? We set them down in front of it all night and then send them to school to find they are both teaching the same God hating crap. That's how that has worked out.

Every occasionally, I think maybe we should have listened to Satan's warnings, he is faithful to warn us but when he offers you an apple you can be sure it has a worm in it. We should know the spirit we are listening to and know its source, then you can know its purpose. Satan is always a liar. Jesus is truth and truth will set you free, but one must walk in him. The Word of God is truth and we are told to study it and meditate on it day and night. It is going to be the final judgment on everything. It is the only thing that can bring two things into one, and we would not need two denominations any more, if we could be brought into one. Like God commanded us to.

We have already covered that, you cannot bring two denominations into one without eliminating one of them. One is one makes one, but one and one makes two every time. Therefore, I am a totally confused, none denominational, and believe entirely in truth. That makes me an enemy to all the evil of the world; and most of the so-called Christians. That is why Jesus said if you are a disciple of mine the world will hate you and lay in wait to kill you at any opportunity. Can you argue with that? I am not bosting on myself, but Jesus. He was the one who said it, and it is all truth, as Obama says, period.

I am totally fed up with people that follow Islam and hold up the Koran as equal to the Bible, and claiming to be a Christian, qualified to tell me what my Bible says. I feel like they are trying to insult what little intelligence I have.

The whole Democrat party, with the old Republican establishment in toe being duped and bought, are not far behind. Completely controlled by Satan, with Obama and Hillary in the driver's seat; are my examples. Hillary, running for president, giving a campaign speech in July, twenty-sixteen, talked on and on, trying to sell herself and her globalist-idealist economy, saying how we had to make room for every person. Everybody in the world should have the same rights. No person should be allowed to suppress another in this world, she has fantasized for us, of course. Her and Bill are the biggest dogs in her world.

You do not have to read far in between the lines to know exactly what she was talking about. She was definitely-talking about; illegal aliens, convicted felons, even convicted terrorist, and don't forget the rioters and gang members and Muslims, and Islam that have vowed to kill all Christians and Jews, until there is no more left on the earth. Even if they must look them up.

We cannot be allowed to offend one of them and to disagree with them is offensive to them. Our Democrat Attorney General has said so. I am sure one of the rights she was talking about is the right to vote in our elections. It was the subject matter in what she was talking about. I have a right to vote, so they must have every right that I have, is what she said. They have already allowed millions of them to vote and have millions more that is in our country now that she was talking about that they have been trying to get registered before the election. They have millions more waiting at our borders they are trying to get in, knowing they will vote 100% a straight Democrat ticket. Bill Clinton pushed through somewhere around two-million shady voters just before his second election, just enough to win. They had them counted before the voting was done. And our government must give them free education, medical access, a welfare check to live on, and I am sure I left out a bunch. How long of a memory do you expect me to have?

There is no way a Democrat will be elected without them and they know it. Election fraud is so common now, they are willing to see you get your head cut off to get themselves elected, especially if you own a gun. They would not have won the last number of elections without millions of completely fraudulent votes.

I do not know about anybody else but I am sick of them. I did not have the stomach to watch their convention. And that is a truth. I named Democrats, God haters, thirty years ago, you had to be careful back then who heard you. But I never was very good at being careful, so I was always in a little trouble. I was talking to a Christian-talking office lady; we already knew that I didn't think much of Democrats and she didn't think much of conservatives. I mentioned that I had named them Democrats, God haters. She about came up out of her chair with, "That's name calling! Where do you get the right to do that?" I ask her, did not Jesus call Herod a fox? And called that one Gentile lady a dog? She agreed; I did not get into the twenty-third chapter of Mathew, full of names he called the Pharisees.

I do not know what Bible most of the other Christians read from, but it is not the same one I read in. I have not voted for a Democrat at the state or national level in well over thirty years and if the Lord allows I do not plan to vote for one in the next thirty years. I do not care if his name is G. Washington. The only reason God put the Muslim Obama in the White House (And he did put him there) for he said he did. He thought he could surely wake up at least a few people in this country.

Carter and Clinton did not wake up very many, so look what he gave us this time. God is making a big effort to wake up his people in this coming election of 2016. Try to hear a few of God's thoughts, and our thoughts about him. He has exposed Obama and Hillary (Two of the biggest Devil possessed lying people across the world) to the entire world. He has our country so close on the edge of the cliff that it is scary to any sane man. You better keep in mind that God is running *everything* if you want to stay with me. So, you ask why did God do that? To try to wake his people up. He even said in his word, "He would plead with us with his wrath." Speaking of these last days.

Them, with a Devil possessed mind, that God has turned over to what he calls a reprobate mind, cannot see it. They hate truth and truth is Jesus. They had rather believe a lie instead, even when they know that it is a lie. And God has told them plainly there will be hell to pay. That is truth and they will not believe it for they hate truth, and love a lie. Read about it in the first chapter of the book to the Romans.

It would be a rare thing to find a person in this country over 16 years old, that does not know that Hillary and Obama are liars, and maybe the biggest liars that ever got into politics. We that are Christians know that Satan is not only a liar but the father of all lies. God has convicted all them that love a lie, speak a lie, help a lie, believe a lie. Now look at yourself (Everybody else is) and tell me that God is your Father? Don't be shocked if I hesitate a little before I believe you. God has told me not to believe a lie, and to try the spirits, they are not all of God. We are responsible for what we believe, plus many other things. I will spare you some of the details, you read your Bible every day surely you can find and read some of them for yourself.

I do not believe that a reprobate minded person, can speak a true statement without at least trying to justify or cover it a bit, with excuses. Like the truth needs justified. With his twisted mind, he thinks it does.

I have run across almost no person that seems to know it, but the Bible says and teaches (In the 2nd chapter of Romans) that the one that is accusing another is guilty of the same thing. I have watched and studied that scripture so long, trying to see it clear through until I am convinced it may be among one of the truest scriptures in the Bible, if there is such a thing. I would like to invite anyone to try it for yourself before you take my word for it. I learned it so well for some years now, I can listen to a liberal politician and tell you *much* about what he is doing; what he is plaining to do; and much about how he is going to try to handle about any situation. It comes by knowing the spirit of a person or thing, this is what I have been writing about. If you know the spirit of something you can just about read it off. Spirits are very true to their source. The Spirit of God will not believe a lie, so no one can lie to God and fool him. Do you think you can?

Man, is easy to fool for he is a fool, God says so. God says not to lean to our own understanding or never to trust in our flesh, nor to depend on our own right arm. Did you ever wonder why? Man, cannot stand up against Satan by himself, he has-to have help from the Spirit of God. If he cannot know the spirits, how can he know what spirit is helping him? To be safe we must develop a communication with God. God has recommended pastors and churches, which is a tremendous idea but they are always short of the spiritually gifted people to help the pastor as God would like. The pastor needs to be the most gifted of them all. He should not take upon himself the responsibility of having all the gifts, but having a gift of discernment, being able to work with all the gifts in the church that are genuine and can flow with the Spirit of God. That will take an especially gifted man, very rare. Therefore, we are all commanded to operate as one body. A church is powerless without unity; so is a country. I have often said I cannot put full confidence in someone who does not have at least a little bit of spiritual discernment and a bunch of fear of God. It only takes one Devil possessed person to break the unity in a whole church. A pastor must be blessed with a certain amount of spiritual wisdom and knowledge, be a very tolerating person, yet realize there is a few things that he cannot tolerate and has not been ask to. Sometimes, it is a demanding pastor that is the biggest problem, so he must have a balanced-out conception of himself. If he has a flaw the Devil will always have somebody there to help him with that; the flaw that is. The Devil is always blessed with, and blessing with, plenty of helpers. That is why you need to know the spirit of anything you are working with. I write that often, in all my books.

Obama did not even qualify to be on the ticket for president, did not even have a birth certificate that he could show, refused to show his school records or any other records. But he had plenty of help getting the job as president. I do not believe one once of it came from the Spirit of God, it didn't need to, but God allowed it to happen. Where was God's people that stood up against it? Anybody that is so openly disrespectful of our countries laws, our Bible, our very foundation that we are built on, our way of life. And you are going to tell me a Christian voted for him and is not duped? I do not see where a Christian has any excuse for voting for him in any office. There is where you can see where the people were that was on God's side and which ones were Devil possessed, or stood on the sidelines and didn't even go to the poles. Do you reckon God was proud of them?

Do you think they were listening to God? Do you think they were the least bit mindful or considerate of our many fore fathers and relatives that gave their lives for what we have here? Maybe you just did not think at all; would that not put you in the category of being dead or asleep?

Now Obama and Clinton, are screaming in the microphones that Trump is not qualified to be president. Reckon which candidate they are talking about? Remember what I said about the one who is accusing?

Didn't take long for me to be able to show it to you. God has done told it to me. If this country does not wake up he is going to give us Hillary, and I just had to agree with him, we will deserve her. You might want to read where Isaiah warned, that in the last days our women would rise and rule over us, our children would become our princes and oppressors.

I just finished reading a list of thirty organizations, that are set up teaching Islam in this country; beside our schools, all other government organizations, news media, and most of our churches. We don't have that many churches that are teaching against it. Muslims are telling across the world how they are going to kill every Christian and Jew from the earth, and doing it at an alarming rate. They have declared war on this nation and killing us, almost if not, daily. And we have not woken up yet. Hypocritical Mystery Babylon Christion's will be the number one target on their list, God has said so.

When God gives us Hillary for a President and the women, queers, criminals, dope heads, gangsters and rioters are cheering, I will be looking for you so called Christians in the middle of them, for that is where you belong. This is the Democrats army, recruited, trained and paid; with our money. I may just cheer a little with you, for it means it is getting much closer for Jesus to be coming back for his own. His own is not going to be a very big group, of course he has already told us that.

With our so called Christian churches teaching we are told to love everything that comes along and give them all the rights that I have, including illegal aliens, and the whole list I just listed a few paragraphs back. Democrats have cut Christians far below all these ones I have named, even court-martialing them and throwing them out of our military for no other reason, but praying in Jesus' name. Some of them locked up in prison for long terms, on nothing but trumped up chargers by Obama's administration. I wish some of them Devil possessed people would read this book. Check it out, if I am lying then come and lock me up. I am not above the law like Hillary and Obama are and I should give them rights above ours, even every right I have? I do not know what Bible they find it in, it just is not in mine. I *do* read where we are supposed to put them, the unbelievers, out from among us and separate ourselves from them. And if one comes unto you bringing any other doctrine beside Jesus and he crucified, to not let him into your house. I could quote a few pages that would back this up. Like, if you give them God speed you will be partakers of their evil deeds. And, "God has no communion with the Devil." God will have no part of a lie in him. Now does that sound like God has commanded everybody to be equal?

They gave out a pole results saying the underage thirty-five year voters favored Hillary by around double the other side. It reminded me of the perfect Christian lady, some time ago, saying, she did not try to influence her children anything about religion. They would just have to make up their own minds as they were growing up, she thought that was fair. That lady had been to school. That is a give up shot if I ever heard one. Does she think the world and Satan is going to be fair and allow her kids to make up their own minds without influence? Satan has done jammed her mind and going to do the same thing to her children. I marvel at the stupidity I hear constantly. Like I keep saying, Satan has possessed our entire teaching system in this country. Listen to Hillary's doctrine, and she wants to build us a free international school for our country to teach everybody to be equal, I see a lot of people I do not care to be equal with, at all.

They like to quote to me, "God says I cannot kill." When that law was given to man it made the total of ten laws that God had given to man. It did not take long to have more laws written to us that did not change any law but sure put some more light on them all to explain them farther. Like establish every word of God from two or three witnesses. I can read to them where God says that if a child cannot be controlled by his parents, to take him before the congregation and let them stone him to death. He said there is a time to kill, and there is a time to make alive, there is a time for everything. Said, if man shed man's blood let his blood be shed by man. My point is Devil possessed people cannot read the Bible, it is Spiritually written and Spiritually discerned. It says to established every word of God from the mouth of two and three witnesses. As I have written in another place all words have at least two meanings. The word kill must have a few dozen or so meanings. What do they know about my Bible when they are Devil possessed? Or how do you kill someone that is already dead?

They like to say that is old testament and done away with, that is another lie from hell. Jesus himself said he did not come to do away with, or change anything about the law, but to fulfill it and bring life to us and more abundantly, which was the Spirit. The Spirit is life and was not given unto man until Jesus took his body back to the Father and they both sent the Spirit back to dwell in each of us that would accept his baptism into it. That is a spiritual thing the carnal cannot see it and cannot have it. The government is now on his shoulders and we cannot bow to an earthly government that is contrary to God's law; only submit to it, that does not mean obey it. And I do not have to submit to it quietly nor blindly. They cannot make a law that you must obey, you can obey or suffer the consequences. Even then, we are to be considered innocent until proven guilty, with a furnished defense. What difference does it make when they are going to cut your head off anyway? It's the kind of law we have now. Did you not hear what Hillary said? "What difference does it make now?"

We have been sold out and divided until we are powerless, Satan has possessed people's, doings, but we have accepted it without a stand. We can either unite or all we can look forward to is judgment. Most of our churches are not preaching the Bible which is Jesus Christ, but Satan's doctrine which is a lie. So, when you are preaching to me, preach the Spirit of God, not Satan; I might just tell you about it. As I have said, I am about filled up with Satan's Bibles and False Prophets. I know the Spirit of God when I am facing it. You see a spirit with your mind, you see and hear carnality with carnal eyes and ears. Jesus said carnal minds are spiritually deaf and blind, maybe you can believe him if you keep reading this book about and from the Bible. Truth kills all evil. (oops, God said not to kill). All lies are evil and contrary to truth. Can you measure the evil in our present politicians? I do not have such a scale, but I believe I would give them an over the top vote.

You can look at the political-correct laws for a start; our Democrat liberal politicians are among the biggest liars on this earth without a doubt. I have been trying to tell them so, for around thirty-five years or longer. They have not been able to have me locked up yet; and was not able to get my church doors closed like they said they was going to. Goodness knows they have tried. Like I have written, they fail to see and cannot admit that God is still running this earth, by the Bible.

He is very angry and we are just starting to feel his wrath. You can be assured it will not pass by unnoticed. I can assure you he has vengeance wrote all over him. That John wrote about in the book of revelations. As I have written, God has not accepted much on limited warfare, he will never compromise truth. We have only one thing to use for a shield, the Spirit of God; which is truth. I can assure anybody they are going to need all of it they can get. We are living in the very last of times, God has reached out toward his people more than any time in his creation. But the demands to all of us must be stronger, as there is becoming fewer of us to carry the load, and the load is getting heavier and heavier. And opposition is getting bigger and bigger. God has said as sin doth abound, grace will more abound. God has not abandon his people, and he never will, but we may have to stand up a little stronger. One and the lord makes a majority ever time. Does not everybody strive to be on the side with the majority and afraid of losing their vote? Better get on the lord's side. I do not fancy the losing side, myself.